TAMING THE PAPER TIGER

To Brad —

With best wishes,

Barbara Hemphill

TAMING THE PAPER TIGER

Organizing the Paper in Your Life

Barbara Hemphill

Dodd, Mead & Company, New York

Library of Congress Cataloging-in-Publication Data

Hemphill, Barbara.
  Taming the paper tiger.

  Includes index.
  1. Paperwork (Office practice)—Management.
2. Filing systems. I. Title.
HF5547.15.H45   1988   651.5   87-30124
ISBN 0-396-09198-9 {PBK.}

*With love to my parents
Everett and Doris Frost
who set a wonderful
example and enabled me
to dream.*

Acknowledgments

I FIRST ADMITTED my dream of writing this book to Florence Feldman in 1982. She has been a constant source of inspiration, support and encouragement. I also owe a great deal of thanks to Carol Smith and Elizabeth Jarrell, who proofed and typed manuscript pages on a moment's notice, to Patricia Hass, who demonstrated her faith in my ideas, and to Susan Gies, whose creativity and humor were invaluable, and to Sasha Georgevitch-Taus for her wonderful illustrations, which bring a smile to my face every time I open the book.

There were literally dozens of clients and friends who contributed to this book, not only with specific paper management ideas, but with continual interest.

Finally, I could never have completed this book without the love and support of my family—my husband, Alfred Taylor, and my children, Jenny, Thoma, and Heidi.

Preface

IT IS MY sincere desire that *Taming the Paper Tiger* will provide ideas to help you solve your paper management problems. I recognize that it is sometimes very difficult to solve any problem by reading a book! In addition to the information available in this book, you will need time and patience. Think of this book as a reference which you can use time and time again through the years, as your changing circumstances require changing systems.

I have tried to write as though you were in the room with me, and we were working together one on one. If, however, as you use this book, you have questions or new ideas, please feel free to write or call me at Barbara Hemphill Associates, 1718 Connecticut Avenue, Suite 410, Washington, D.C. 20009. (202) 387-8007. I am certain that together we can tame *your* paper tiger!

Contents

Introduction

WHETHER YOU ARE male or female, young or old, make $10,000 a year and live in a studio apartment, or make $100,000 a year and live on a ten-acre estate, you are, or will be, deluged with paper.

As an organizing consultant, I have spent thousands of hours dealing with people and their paper, from parents struggling with the piles of papers their kids bring home from school to corporation executives responsible for thousands of files. One fact is absolutely clear: paper management skills are essential for survival in our society.

The sheer volume of mail that confronts us daily demands increased skills in paper management. Compare the amount of mail in your mailbox today with that of five years ago. Although the computer age was billed as the "paperless age," it didn't take any of us long to realize that, although the computer does eliminate some piles of paper, it also creates even larger piles. In case you have any doubts about how the computer has affected your life, change your middle initial the next time you sign your name on a catalog order. Then keep track of the additional mail generated as a result of signing your name once. One client tried this and counted over 100 pieces in less than twelve months!

Just deciding what to do with the catalogs is a major issue in many households. Our fascination with sleek, alluring ads for products to improve our appearance, reduce our workload, or please our family, plus our inability to decide whether we are buying or browsing, adds up to piles of catalogs in numerous places around the house. And don't forget all those magic money-making offers! Rarely a week goes by without the arrival of at least one "Have we got a deal for you!"

Then there is the copy machine. Many of us have easy access to a machine in our workplace, at the local library, or even at the neighborhood quick food shop. We cut out articles, advertisements, recipes, and reviews we think will interest a family member or a friend, and make a copy—and an extra, just in case!

Then we have to decide what to do with our own copy, and how to get the other copies to the intended destinations. Unless you have a system to accomplish that task easily, the results over a period of months or years can be devastating: piles and shopping bags full of "good intentions" stuffed under beds and in closets; boxes stacked in the attic or basement; and drawers, badly needed for current storage of essentials, filled instead with unidentified papers.

Another complicating factor in the management of paper in the twentieth century is the basic change in family lifestyle. In the old days, Papa sat down at his desk at the end of each month to pay the bills. He probably never had more than five or six in a busy month! Nowadays, with the advent of "plastic money," the number of bills to pay each month has increased overwhelmingly. Today, in single parent families, or with both parents working, the time for paper shuffling is limited, but the amount of paper to shuffle seems unlimited: child care arrangements, car pool schedules, travel itineraries, shopping lists, school permission slips, house repair "to do" lists, and piles of career-related magazines and newspapers to read. Support from family members, and from household and personal services, is vital, but using it effectively requires good paper management skills.

"Blended families"—those with children from more than one marriage—can also create special paper management challenges. If you need to give your son some information or take him to buy soccer shoes, but you only see him on Tuesday night, you need a paper management system that makes you see "Buy soccer shoes" on Tuesday. It won't help to see it on Monday or Wednesday.

I grew up on a farm. As a young girl learning to cook, I remember discovering very quickly that making one or two dishes was quite simple. Even though I knew how to make every dish on the menu, the hard part was getting them all on the table at the same time, with the potatoes and gravy still hot and the salad still cold. That was the real challenge. Paper management requires the same skill.

Most people know how to do the majority of the individual tasks required in personal paper management—paying bills, writing letters, filing papers, etc. The difficult part is getting it all done at the right time. To accomplish that requires a comprehensive system.

This book will provide guidelines to help you to fill in the gaps in your paper management system, or to develop a totally new one, if you feel it is necessary.

Developing a personal paper management system takes motivation, time, and practice. If you have been shuffling the same piles of paper on the kitchen counter for months, or even years, it can be frightening to change. Accept this as a normal reaction, not an indication that you are doing something wrong.

Digging through a pile of papers can be somewhat like waking a tiger who is temporarily asleep. We discover papers that represent disappointments, obligations, uncertainty, indecision, and the blinding reality that we are not able to do all the things we want to or think we ought to. Just as we have a temporary respite when the tiger sleeps, we have a temporary respite when we ignore the papers, but constantly in the back of our minds is the fear that the tiger will awake at any moment.

The results of organizing the paper in your life will be more than just an uncluttered counter. As one client put it, "I was so preoccupied with finding my way through the forest that I didn't notice the trees. Organizing my paper made it easier for me to identify what is important in my life." An effective paper management system will help you control what you do with your time and energy and create an environment that is supportive of your plans and dreams.

I do not believe that we ever set goals that are too high. Rather, we often allow too little time to reach them. Learning paper management skills takes time, like learning any other skill, but you can do it! And it will be worth the effort!

1

The Roar of the Tiger

CAN YOU RECOGNIZE this scene? You sit down to pay some bills. You vaguely remember that the electric bill needs to be paid, but you can't remember where you put it. Your son comes in to tell you he needs his birth certificate the next day to prove he's old enough for driving lessons. Where is it? Your friend calls to ask if you're free on the eighteenth for a get-together. That date stands out in your mind for some reason. You think maybe there's a notation on your calendar at work, but there's nothing on your home calendar.

You feel a headache coming on. There are piles of bills, junk mail, and catalogs all over your desk and night table and it almost seems to grow right before your eyes!

What you're experiencing is the roar of the tiger—the paper tiger.

It may feel like he is out of control, that the situation is hopeless. The truth is, you can stop this pattern—tame that tiger—with a powerful tool: a paper management system.

Paper management is a tool to help you accomplish

what is important to you, whether it is finding your birth certificate when you need it, paying your bills on time, having all the papers you need when you go to your tax accountant, submitting insurance claims within the time limit, or keeping track of your frequent flyer miles.

There is Hope For You, Too

Paper management means developing a system that fits your personal needs. No matter who you are and what your paper management challenges may be, there is a way for you to improve the way you handle paper—one that you create yourself for your own particular needs and life-style. You may know how to handle a particular paper problem, but for various reasons you have not done so. Before long, the paper gets lost in the shuffle of more papers. You become so bogged down in all this paper that you end up not taking the appropriate action to end the vicious cycle.

Success in paper management requires four ingredients:

1. Positive attitude
2. Sufficient time
3. Appropriate skills
4. Adequate maintenance

If any component of the system is weak or missing, the system will begin to break down. Nine times out of ten, when a system breaks down, it is an indication of a changing situation, not a bad system. Perhaps the amount of paper has grown, the support system has changed, or the objectives have been revised.

You've Got to Think Positive

A "positive attitude" as it relates to paper management is an essential prerequisite. It is important for you to expect that, with the help of this book, you can and will develop a system for yourself that will suit your particular needs.

One of the most exciting aspects of being an organizing consultant is helping people create a system to fit their specific needs, and seeing their sense of relief when they realize how much simpler their lives can be. Frequently people procrastinate about doing anything with the paper in their lives, because they are waiting to find the "right" way.

There *is* no "right" or "wrong" way! Many times I set up systems for other people that I personally would find very frustrating. As you read this book, you will discover that there are many styles of paper management. Don't worry about how other people do it. Just look for techniques that work for you!

To foster your positive attitude about paper management, recognize that any system you develop is a *tool* to help *you* do what *you* want or need to do. A friend of mine says, "I hate jogging; I love having jogged!" Paperwork is like that in many ways. Few people, if any, like doing it, but taking the time to set up a system means spending less time shuffling paper and more time enjoying the results—in short, taming the paper tiger.

Tomorrow and Tomorrow and Tomorrow

How many times have you said to yourself: "I'll do it when things calm down . . . ," "when the kids go back to school . . . ," "when the kids get out of school . . . ," "when the guests leave . . . ," "when I come home from my business trip . . . ," "when the house is remodeled." "I'll do it as soon as I have a block of time—this weekend maybe, or over the holidays." "I know . . . when I'm on vacation . . . or when I retire . . . tomorrow."

But the weekend, the holidays, the vacations come and go. As soon as one crisis is over (and sometimes before!), the next one begins. And the cycle goes on. Before you know it, you have a desk full of letters you really intended to answer, ten months of health insurance claims to submit, the attic and the basement are filled with magazines that never got read while they were in the den (but that have wonderful articles and recipes in them!), and it's April 10th, and you have no idea where your income tax forms are stashed! Many a client has called after being retired several months, or even years, saying, "I still don't have the time."

If you wait "until things calm down" before you begin to do something about the paper tiger in your life, it could be a very long wait.

Decide to Decide

There is a very simple axiom regarding paper: Paper clutter is postponed decisions; paper management is decision making.

Papers pile up on our counters, tables, and desks because there are decisions we need to make about them. "Do I really need to keep this letter from my lawyer about my father's estate?" "How long should I keep the bank statements from the account I closed three years ago?" "Where should I keep my will?" "What do I do with all those family photographs my mother gave me for safekeeping?" "How can I find that recipe I saw in *Gourmet* magazine when I want it?" "What should I do with health insurance statements?" "Where do I put the instructions from the new garage door opener?"

Every time you ask one of these questions without making a decision—a reply—and then taking the appropriate action, you have left some unsettled business. Postpone a few of the decisions, and a new pile is born.

Four Questions to Ask

Each of these questions can be categorized as one of four basic questions:

1. Do I *really* need to keep this?
2. *Where* should I keep it?
3. How *long* should I keep it?
4. How can I *find* it?

Each one of these questions requires a decision to be made. But many, many people run into trouble here. Just why are these decisions so difficult for us to make? There are two major reasons—lack of information and fear of failure.

Information Please

Unfortunately, even though paper management is an essential skill in the twentieth century, few people have had an opportunity to learn paper management skills in a formal way. It simply is not taught.

The purpose of this book is to help you recognize the paper management problems in your life, to motivate you to do something about them, and to provide you with the tools to find solutions and develop systems. If you are having problems with a specific paper area, check the table of contents and read the chapter that applies to that particular area. Each chapter is complete within itself. You do not need to read the entire book to be able to put it to work for you, but do read the entire chapter before you begin trying a new system. Use this as a reference book, not only when you are first setting up a system, but to refer to as you outgrow existing systems, and find you need to make revisions.

But . . . What If?

The second major reason people have difficulty making decisions is fear. You are afraid that your decision will be proven wrong, that you will regret the decision you made, or that someone will be disappointed or hurt by your decision. You ask yourself: "What if I get audited by the IRS and I don't have what I need?" "What if I throw something away and it turns out to be very valuable?" "What if my children want or need this information someday?" "What if I file this important document and then I can't find it?"

It is not easy to answer the "what ifs" correctly, and all of you know of someone, or have had an experience in your own life, that has proven that, every once in a while, you end up needing something you once threw out. But here are the facts: 1) if your paper tiger is big enough, you can't find most of your paper anyway; and 2) *almost* everything *is* replace-able. You can probably get another copy if you really need to, and, if you don't *really* need to, then it prob-ably wasn't worth the clutter it would have caused in the first place. Remember Hemphill's Principle: "If you don't know you have it, or you can't find it, it is of NO value to you!"

No Magic in Insight

Suppose you can take the time to set up a system, and you know what you need to do, but you just don't want to do it? What then?

There is no magic in insight! Just because you know there is a better way, doesn't mean you will do it. You need to take action on your insight. I know that if I exercise at least twenty minutes a day, three times a week, I will feel better, look better, and live longer—but that does not make me ride my bicycle or jog with my daughter.

In fact, we frequently do not act on our insights, until a crisis forces us to do so. We become concerned about our eating habits when the doctor says our life is at risk if we do not. We decide to do something about a messy desk when we recognize that it doesn't work for us anymore. One client decided to do some-thing about his paper tiger when the penalty on his overdue inheritance tax bill became larger than his annual income and he was threatened with jail! What price are you willing to pay before you act?

Ultimately, you will have to make the decision to tame the tiger yourself. The most I can do is point out how chaotic the alternative is. No doubt you know that already, or you wouldn't be reading this. *Taming the Paper Tiger* will give you answers to questions and guidelines to use that will help you form your own system for managing the paper tiger in your life. The rest is up to you.

2

Get Centered

YOU ARRIVE HOME from work or from the afternoon soccer carpool feeling exhausted and rushed to
get to a 7:30 p.m. meeting. You grab the mail out of
the box and drink a quick cup of coffee while you
glance at it.

You begin making piles on the kitchen table: one
for trash, because there isn't a wastebasket within
reach, one for bills you need to pay, another for things
you want to read, etc. Just then the phone rings. You
answer it. By the time you finish your conversation,
it is time to prepare dinner. You scoop everything up—
trash and all, since there isn't time to determine which
pile is which—and put it in the bay window. That's
Monday.

On Tuesday you sit down in the family room to
read the mail. The children are watching TV, and you
want to spend a little time with them before dinner.
The routine is the same. You get distracted. But this
time the pile goes on the coffee table. On Wednesday, it's the table beside the bed, because you want
to talk to your spouse before the business trip.

By the end of the week, you have six piles of mail around the house, half-opened, half-read, and cluttering every room. But you can't find the bill you planned to pay yesterday, or the tickets you need for the game tonight!

The first step in solving the paper management problem at home is to establish a location where you will routinely handle all paperwork. If you want to tame that tiger, you have to start by putting him in a cage.

I strongly urge you to set up a *permanent* center for your paperwork that will be available to you at *all* times. At seminars I give for managing paper at the office, one of the most frequent comments I hear from participants is, "It's even worse at home!" I ask them, "Where do you do your paperwork at home?" Typically, the response is "sometimes here . . . sometimes there." Therein lies a major part of the problem!

Just taking your mail to a central place will eliminate scattered piles of paper, misplaced bills and checks, and forgotten notices. One class participant was amazed at how much easier her life became once she set up a desk area in the kitchen equipped with a telephone and a file cabinet.

"How can that be so important?" you may ask. Have you ever tried to repot a plant in the kitchen sink using a tablespoon because you didn't feel like going to the basement to get the proper tool? Have you tried to scrub the whitewalls on your tires with a sponge because you didn't have the proper cleanser and didn't have time to go to the store to get it? It's no different from the many times you opened an invitation to a party that you wouldn't think of missing, but procrastinated about RSVP-ing because the telephone was in the other room. Have you mailed a bill a week later than you planned to because you kept forgetting to buy stamps?

When I was a child growing up on a Nebraska farm, my father used to tell me that half of the battle in getting any job done is having the right tool. The same is true in paper management.

Choose Your Paper Place

The first step is to choose a comfortable place to handle your papers. If you like sunshine or have allergies to mold, the basement, for example, is not likely to be satisfactory. If you like to be in the mainstream of family activity, the family room may be an excellent location. Perhaps you are easily distracted. Then an out-of-the-way bedroom will probably work better. If you have small children, set up your work center in

Having the right tool may be all you need...

an area where they can play while you work. Do whatever you can to make it a place you like to be. Get a radio if you like music; put a cushion on your chair; or get a new lamp to put on your desk. Paperwork under the best of circumstances is not much fun, and you will not be encouraged to do it if you dislike your work area. Many people prefer to use the kitchen or dining room table, or because of space constraints, have no other option. *However, if at all possible, establish a permanent location that can be left alone.* You do not want to have to constantly interrupt the billpaying process in order to set the table for dinner.

One client had four desks, and *none* of them worked. Her first assignment was to choose the one she liked most, get some boxes, and empty it entirely. From that point, we started over to make not only a desk that she liked, but a desk that worked!

Obviously, many of the decisions you make regarding your work area will be based on how much room you have in your home. But even if your space is limited, there are numerous possibilities. A butcher block top or a piece of plywood placed across two filing cabinets will create a nice size work area, and provide plenty of file space for the average home. The biggest disadvantage to this arrangement is a lack of a small drawer for supplies such as paper clips, stamps, pens, etc. You can purchase a file cabinet with two small drawers and one filing drawer. If they cost more than you want to pay, use a plastic caddy designed to carry tools or cleaning supplies to hold your desk supplies, or something more dramatic, such as acrylic, wood, or brass.

A Desk is a Desk is a Desk?

Does it matter what type of desk or desk arrangement you designate for your work center? Yes, very much so. Some desks simply do not *work* for you. The key word is "functional."

Many homes have desks that are lovely to look at and horrible to use. A rolltop desk, for example, while very beautiful, is difficult for most people to use, because of the limited work space, and the numerous small "cubbyholes" that soon become catch-alls for unidentified papers. If you are going to use such a desk, be sure to label the various compartments: one for envelopes, one for postcards, one for stamps, and so on.

Some people love those beautiful secretary desks— love to look at them, that is. The biggest disadvantage to this type is its small size. The best way to use this kind of desk is to designate it for a particular paper project, such as personal correspondence. If you are particularly fond of the desk or it has sentimental significance, this will be an advantage. You will like to go there, and you are, therefore, more inclined to write personal letters. Keep all your note stationery there, or at least a supply of any different styles you may use, as well as any greeting cards you have purchased. Put letters you want to answer in one spot. When the pile starts to build up, you know it is time to make an appointment with yourself to write letters. Put your favorite picture postcards there as well. You will be able to answer a letter, write a quick thank you note, or send a birthday card in the five minutes you have before the taxi comes, or before you drive the carpool.

Set Up Your Center

Wherever you choose to make your work area, be sure you have adequate lighting and a comfortable chair. One client and I spent a considerable amount of time setting up her paper management system. She understood it and liked it, yet she never seemed to get things done—until we discovered another problem. Her arthritic neck always hurt when she sat at the desk. As soon as we purchased an adjustable chair, the neckache disappeared.

If you want to be able to move around in your work area, you will find a swivel chair on rollers a big advantage. If there is carpeting, you will need an acrylic chair mat.

A major factor in managing paper is an effective filing system. (For detailed discussion, see Chapter 10.) A file cabinet is one of the best investments you will ever make. It is ideal if your filing system is located close to your work center. There is a variety of filing equipment on the market, other than the traditional file cabinet, ranging from inexpensive cardboard boxes to costly acrylic file cabinets on rollers, which you can move to the area you are working. These are found in office furniture stores and mail order catalogs.

If you plan to type and you can afford the space, leave your typewriter out at all times. Often it takes longer to get out the typewriter than it does to type the letter!

If you have a computer, decide whether it should be located in your work area or someplace else, so that you can still work while other members of the family use the computer.

Have a telephone within easy reach at your work area, even if it means putting a 25-foot cord on the phone in the next room, or buying a cordless phone.

You will be amazed at how many pieces of paper you can eliminate immediately by making a phone call when you first open your mail. If you are right-handed, you will probably want the phone on your left, so you are free to write while talking on the phone. If you are short on desk space, consider a wall phone, but be sure to get one with the buttons and the on/off switch on the handset so you can still use it while sitting at your desk. A speaker phone option is particularly useful if you like to do other tasks while talking on the phone or when you get put "on hold." You may also want to use an answering machine (See Chapter 18).

Designate a special place to put those items that are ready to go to the mailbox or the post office. A napkin holder works well and can add to the personality of your work space. I use a beautifully handcrafted ceramic one, which I purchased on a vacation and which evokes pleasant memories each time I look at it.

You will also need a "To Sort" tray (See Chapter 4) located on or within easy reach of your desk to collect the papers that require your action when you are ready to work.

Other pieces of equipment you may find helpful are a calculator, a postage scale, and a bulletin board. Be careful about that last one! For many people it simply becomes a catch-all for postponed decisions. To avoid that, identify it for a specific purpose, such as upcoming invitations, greeting cards, or other mementos you've received (to be changed when they become tired-looking), messages to family members, or an envelope system for credit card receipts and bank deposit records. (See Chapter 12).

Last, but not least, a *large* wastebasket is one of the most important tools in your work area. I cannot ex-

plain why, but I observe that people are more likely to use a large wastebasket than a small one, so choose carefully!

The Essentials

Once you have all the major equipment you need, concentrate on getting the necessary desk supplies. Nothing is more frustrating than to discover you can't staple your resume together because you've run out of staples, or to find a bill you thought was paid a week ago buried in the bottom of your purse or briefcase, because you didn't have a stamp when you needed it!

This list of essentials should satisfy most of your needs:

Calendar (See Chapter 6)
Carbon paper
Correction fluid (for pen and xerox copy)
Dictionary
Envelopes
File folders, manila (See Chapter 9)
Hole punch

Index Cards
Labels, plain and preprinted return address labels
Letter opener
Paper clips
Pencil sharpener (a good-quality one!)
Pens, pencils, marking pens
Postcards, stationery, notepaper
"Post-It" Notes
Rolodex or phonebook (See Chapter 8)
Rubber bands
Scissors
Scotch tape and dispenser
Stamps
Stapler, staples, staple remover
If you have a typewriter:
Correction fluid (if typewriter not self-correcting)
Ribbons and correcting ribbon, if needed
If you have a computer:
Instruction manuals
Storage and program disks

Be careful not to accumulate excess clutter, such as pens that don't write well, paper weights you don't like or use, or drawers full of forgotten or unidentifiable objects. If you find more things in your desk that you don't use than you do, start over! Get a box and empty the contents of your desk into them, keeping only those items you use or enjoy seeing in your work area.

If you have everything you feel you will need, the first step on the road to effective paper management is complete. Congratulations! That tiger will be purring in no time.

3

Taming the Tiger: The Paper Management System

YOU HAVE DRAWERS full of unidentified papers, shopping bags under the bed, boxes of papers stuffed in the closet, or perhaps you haven't eaten on the dining room table for a week because of the papers piled there. You want to end this vicious cycle, and you're encouraged by what you've read so far. (Yes, there is hope for you, too!) But, you may be wondering where to begin.

Who's Controlling Who?

Although a clean desk is not important or necessary to everyone, the ability to find information when you need it is. Perhaps you are afraid that if you clean off your desk or kitchen counter, you will forget what it is you need to do or never be able to find the papers again. Have you ever been late to that big game because the tickets were not where you thought they were and you had to spend fifteen minutes looking for them? If that is the case, then the paper is controlling you, instead of you controlling the paper.

The solution to this problem is a paper management system. But how do you develop such a system?

A cluttered desk indicates a pattern of postponed decisions. The paper management system described in the next seven chapters will assist you in deciding where your paper should go. If you use this system, you will be able to accomplish the objectives of an effective paper management system, which are to:

1. Eliminate unnecessary paper.
2. Avoid generating unnecessary paper.
3. Establish a location for essential paper.
4. Create a method of easy retrieval of paper.

When you have no paper management system or when the system you do have is not working satisfactorily, the unavoidable problems of paper in the twentieth century are compounded. You soon discover that you are writing notes about notes you have already written, because you are afraid you won't find the first one! Your calendar is bulging with notices of special events you are thinking of going to, but fail to find until the event is over. You spend hours looking for that crucial piece of paper that you know you put someplace special, but end up calling to get a duplicate because it is nowhere to be found.

Forget About the Backlog

When I first started as an organizing consultant and was faced with a huge backlog of client's papers, I thought that I should work with the client to eliminate that backlog first, and then develop a system for them. It didn't take long to realize that paper management means developing a system to stop feeling guilty over yesterday's pile and do something about today's.

Here is an example that applies to many people—photographs. Instead of wasting your energy berating yourself every time you open the closet door and see those boxes of photographs, decide what action you can take to stop the cycle, and then do it! One client handled this particular paper problem by not bringing the photographs home until she had taken certain steps at her office. First, she threw away any photographs that she did not like for one reason or another. (Keep in mind that even professional photographers use only a small percentage of the photos they take.) Next, she dates the photos and makes any necessary notations on them. (She has to be careful with this step, and not allow it to become an overwhelming one, causing her to procrastinate about the project altogether! She has made a commitment to herself that the date is the only absolute requirement.) Next, she has her secretary prepare a pile of heavy envelopes addressed to her parents and her in-laws. Because her favorite photo-processing store charges very little for duplicate prints, she orders them automatically. (If you do not order duplicates, but have some photos you want to duplicate, designate an envelope for those negatives which you need to return to the store for duplicating.) Whatever duplicates she does not send to her family and friends she throws away immediately. This not only minimizes the number of photographs she has to deal with at home, but it pleases the grandparents immensely.

Finally, she puts the remaining photographs into the plastic pages that the photo-processing store gives her when she pays for the pictures. All she has to do when she gets home is put the pages in a looseleaf notebook. One of the extra bonuses resulting from this solution is that other members of her family have become much more interested in the photos, because they are easily visible instead of buried in boxes in the closet!

This particular paper problem was a continual frustration. She decided to come up with a system to correct it—one that fit her needs and circumstances—and that is exactly what she did. She has since applied such systems to other paper problems, with success. She didn't think she had the discipline to do it, but she did. And you can too.

The Magnificent Seven

In my experience, every piece of paper in your life can be managed effectively by putting the piece of paper, or the information on it, into one of seven places:

1. "To Sort" Tray
2. Wastebasket
3. Calendar/s
4. "To Do" List
5. Rolodex/Phone Book
6. Action Files
7. Reference Files

Perhaps you're saying to yourself, "That's far too regimented for me. I could never do that!"

The fact is you can. I've worked with dozens of clients who said the same thing.

It's important to keep in mind the benefits of using the system. Imagine how it will feel to be able to clean off the kitchen counter when company is coming, and know that you will be able to find the credit card bill again tomorrow, or to be able to spend two minutes retrieving the directions to a friend's house, instead of fifteen minutes trying to reach your friend to get them again.

You will discover not only that it is possible to control the paper in your life, but the rewards greatly enhance the quality of your daily life.

Remember that today's mail is tomorrow's pile. Take today's mail to your paper management center, and begin now to develop your own paper management system.

4

To Sort It Out

ONE OF THE major stumbling blocks for many people in managing their paper is deciding where to begin. One day you look at the top of the desk and decide that the situation has gone far enough. You are tired of looking at the piles of paper and spending hours looking for important information. So you start with one pile, but before long, you find something you don't feel like doing or can't do for one reason or another. So you go to another pile and start again. The same thing happens. Before you know it, three hours have passed and the only thing that has changed is the clock, which said 9:00 when you began and now says 12:00. You feel even more discouraged!

For now, ignore all those old piles. The time will come to deal with them, and you will become more skilled at doing it as you practice.

To Sort Short

Begin by putting today's mail, or whatever pile of papers you wish to organize, into your "To Sort" tray.

Many people refer to this as their "In Box," but I shy away from the term. Often people are not clear about the meaning of "In," and I find mail weeks or even years old in the bottom of the "In Box." Soon it becomes a hiding place for undesirable tasks. Do not feel that the "To Sort" tray has to be a tray. A box, bin, basket, shelf, or just a designated spot on a desk or table will do nicely.

The "To Sort" tray is a temporary spot for papers that you have not yet identified (sorted out), i.e., the mail you grabbed out of the box, the papers given to you by other members of the family, the papers picked up at a meeting or taken out of your own briefcase (in fact, you may need to have a "To Sort" on each floor of your home to transport papers from purses, pockets, drawers, etc. to your desk for action).

"Well," you say, "there's nothing so special about

that. I already have sixteen 'To Sort' piles all around the house. There's even one in the bathroom! I'm very good at 'To Sort' piles!" Here's where the discipline comes in. To make the 'To Sort' tray work for you, you must learn to:

1) Sort short. Be prepared to keep your papers in this temporary resting spot a short time only.

2) Use your "To Sort" spot consistently.

The trick to changing your habits and making this system work is to do the sorting frequently, before the next pile begins. Your "To Sort" tray is *the* place for papers to rest until you can get to the sorting. If it is becoming a permament home, you are not sorting often enough.

Handle Once?

You may have heard the expression, "Handle a piece of paper only once." For the majority of the people I know, this is impossible. I think it *is* possible and desirable, however, to handle a piece of paper only once more after it has been placed in the "To Sort" tray. Remember: The "To Sort" tray is a temporary resting place. The paper should stay there just long enough for you to determine what you need to do with it next. In some cases, it will go directly into the wastebasket (See Chapter 5) or you will want to take immediate action, so one handling will be enough. But in many cases, you will move it from "To Sort" into another part of your paper management system. Chapters 6, 7, 8, 9, and 10 describe in detail the five places your paper might belong in the system.

5

Mastering the Art of Wastebasketry

THE NEXT STEP is to eliminate any paper that is easily identifiable as unnecessary. The "art of wastebasketry" is undoubtedly one of the most essential skills to learn and use for effective paper management, since our lives are glutted with paper—newspapers, magazines, mail order catalogs, bills, requests for donations, cancelled checks, memos, reminders, invitations, school papers, personal correspondence, and probably the most frustrating of all, "junk mail."

Enough is Enough

Each day brings a world of opportunities—frequent flyer bonus offers, entertainment and educational opportunities, information about new services and stores, magazines with wonderful recipes and entertaining ideas. But in order to take advantage of any of these, you need to be able to retrieve the appropriate information at the right moment. Uncontrolled information is not a resource, but a burden. Piles of magazines with interesting, informative articles soon become dust collectors that take up space and create guilt. A collection of information on health and exercise equipment soon takes up as much space as an exercise bicycle, but does nothing to help you increase stamina or lose weight.

It is not accidental that the wastebasket occurs at the top end of the paper management system! Research shows that 80% of the paper we collect is never used! My years with people and their paper have convinced me that your ability to achieve goals is directly related to your willingness to use the wastebasket. And there is no doubt that your stress level in the long run will decrease as the amount of paper in your wastebasket increases.

Whenever you place an order from a catalog or request information about a product or a service, you can be certain your name will be passed on to other companies. Even the telephone directory companies sell mailing lists! (If you have difficulty throwing away "junk mail" or would prefer not to have to, contact your local post office for the address you can write to to remove your name from multiple mailing lists. Also, be aware that many applications and order forms contain a box you can check if you do not wish to be put on the other mailing lists.) In all likelihood, the overwhelming majority of papers you receive in the mail will *eventually* end up in the garbage, anyway. The issue is whether or not they will first be allowed to collect dust in your home.

Five Guidelines for Answering "Do I Really Need This?"

This is where you've got to learn to get tough. Take each piece of paper and analyze it by asking each of these questions. This may be difficult at first. But after a while, you'll run through the five questions instantaneously, *and* you will actually begin to enjoy throwing papers out. I play a game with myself to see how many papers I can get in the wastebasket before they even make it to the desk! Here are the questions to ask yourself:

1. *Is this only for my information, and now I know it?* Much of the information we receive is sent to us automatically because of computer mailing lists, or friends or relatives send us articles they think might interest us.
2. *Does this information exist elsewhere?* Is it in a book you already have? For example, information about taking care of geraniums might also be in a book you already have on plant care. Would it be easy enough to get it in the library if you decided you really needed it? Do you have an audio or video tape with the same information?
3. *Is the information recent enough to be useful?* A two-year-old restaurant directory is of extremely limited value.
4. *Under what circumstances would you want this information?* "Just in case" is not a sufficient answer. If you cannot identify how you would use the

information, it is unlikely that you would re-member that you have it, or be able to find it. Keep in mind Hemphill's Principle: *"If you don't know you have it, or you can't find it, it is of no value to you."*

5. *Finally, what is the worst possible thing that could happen if you didn't have this piece of paper?* If you are willing to live with the consequences, toss it immediately!

Remember: Always open your mail next to the "cir-cular file"—the wastebasket. It will make it easier for you to toss things out, and throwing the paper on the floor beside you would only make extra work! Always ask yourself, "Do I really need or want to keep this?"

In the first few months of my career as an organiz-ing consultant, I was hired by a highly respected professional to organize her condominium. You can-not imagine my shock when I opened the door to see piles of paper, several feet deep, surrounded by small piles of paper, which were obviously multiple at-tempts to "get organized." Before long, she confessed that she had finally succumbed to calling me because, when the condominium association sent someone to do a routine spraying for insects, he reported that her home had been ransacked! Since that incident, I have met dozens of people who have not had guests in their homes for years, because they were too embar-rassed by their piles of paper. Don't let that happen to you.

6

Your Calendar

YOUR CALENDAR IS one of your most important organizing tools. It is a major key to effective time management and a major factor in effective paper management, as well.

You can eliminate a surprising number of pieces of paper from the piles on your desk simply by using your calendar. The key here is to get into the habit of extrapolating the information you need from the paper, entering it on your calendar, and then throwing out the pieces of paper or filing it away.

The Working Calendar

Here's how it works. Let's say you receive a meeting notice in the mail. Frequently you can enter the information—time, place, telephone number for further information—directly into your calendar. Then you can throw the notice away. If there is more essential information on the notice than what will fit in your calendar, such as an agenda, directions, etc., you can note the name of the meeting in your calendar, and put the notice itself into "Hold" (See Chapter 9). Put an Ⓗ beside the notation in your calendar, so you will know that further information can be found in "Hold." Be careful not to put *so* much information into your calendar that it becomes unreadable!

Suppose you read in the newspaper about a concert you would like to go to, if you get home from work in time, and if there are no other family obligations. Put it on your calendar—in pencil—both on the day you need to respond and on the day of the event. If you find there is more than one possibility for a particular time slot, you can then make a conscious choice about what you will do, instead of reacting to whichever notice happens to wend its way to the top of the pile. If you simply leave the notice on your desk so that you won't forget, you are likely to handle that piece of paper dozens of time. But if it doesn't resurface on the appropriate day, you have accomplished nothing — except unnecessary paper shuffling!

If you've written a letter to someone, and you need to get a reply in two weeks, make a note to yourself in your calendar, "Heard from John?" Use your calendar not only as an appointment calendar, but as a tool for effective follow-up. If there are specific materials here you want to remember to check when you follow up, make a note of that directly in your calendar.

Make an Appointment with Yourself

In my experience, the people who are most successful in managing their time and accomplishing their goals are those who make appointments with themselves to complete specific tasks, and to remind themselves to check on specific issues. For example, let's say you are at a meeting, and you agree to complete a certain task. Instead of writing a note to yourself on the legal pad you are carrying with you, make a quick calculation about when you need to begin work on that task, and write a note to yourself in your calendar. In this way you avoid creating additional pieces of paper, and you will be reminded at exactly the right time.

If there is a specific task you need to do for yourself (for example, clean out your file drawer, or spend some time on your "To Read" pile; See Chapter 16), make an appointment with yourself, just as you would with someone else.

Some people are hesitant to use this approach, because they are afraid of becoming too compulsive. They shudder to think of themselves talking to a friend and having to say, "I need to go now. I have to catch up on my reading!" I am not suggesting such inflexibility! Using your calendar as a time management tool helps you to be *realistic* about your time. If you have blocked out an hour to write the minutes from your last committee meeting, and you decide you would rather do something else, or you have to take your child to the doctor, you can realistically decide on your options for that given day. Perhaps you can write the minutes while you are waiting at the doctor's office, or perhaps you need to block out another time later in the week. Having both items written down on the calendar will enable you to plan in advance exactly what you can and cannot accomplish.

Choose Your Calendar Wisely

In actually choosing your calendar, there are several factors to consider. If you use your calendar as I've described, you will need to choose a calendar with plenty of writing space. Of course, this will mean a larger size calendar, and, if you do not regularly carry a purse or a briefcase, you may feel this is not practical, and you will have to make adjustments. One alternative is to use the "Post-It" Notes, which can be easily affixed to your calendar, and removed when you have completed the tasks, to give you additional writing space.

A second factor to consider in choosing your calendar is the format. Do you need to see the year at a glance, the month, each day, or a combination? I like a combination. My calendar has a year-at-a-glance in the front on which I record key words to tell me what city I will be in, or what the major "non-negotiable" appointment is for the day—appointments, major events, travel schedules, etc. The next section is a page-a-day, with the page divided into sections—one section for fixed appointments with myself or with someone else, and one section for my daily "To Do" list, which can be squeezed in between appointments or during blocks of time when I have no specific appointments. The third small section provides space to note tax deductible expenses. This format is particu-

sasha

larly pleasing to Uncle Sam! (See back of book for order form.)

Is One Calendar Enough?

If your business and personal life overlap, as they do in my case, your best option might be a master calendar that reflects both areas of your life. In this case, it will be important to carry your calendar with you most of the time.

If your business life is basically "nine to five," then you will need a master calendar at the office. You will also need a master calendar for your personal life, and you might need to take it with you to the office, since most people end up doing personal business sometime during the work day.

Say a colleague asks, "Why don't you join me for a tennis game Saturday afternoon?" You can check your calendar and give an immediate answer (unless you need to check with other family members). If you do not have your personal calendar at the office, immediately you have created more work for yourself, because you will have to go home and check your calendar. Chances are when you return the call to make final arrangements, your friend will be out, and the familiar game of telephone tag begins!

Another alternative is to carry a small calendar with you that reflects major events from both calendars. The hassle with this approach, of course, is that you will need to record appointments (with yourself as well as with others!) in two calendars instead of one. The hazard is that if you fail to do that, you will miss something important.

The question that you may be asking is "How important *is* it to carry my calendar with me?" Certainly you will have to weigh the alternatives for yourself.

If you do not already carry a calendar with you, one way to determine this is to keep track for several days of how many times you would have referred to your calendar if you had had it with you.

In addition to your master calendar or calendars, you may need other calendars for specific functions. Don't get caught in the trap of having more calendars than you can manage, however. The key to the success of more than one calendar is to identify clearly the specific purpose of each. For example, many families find it crucial to hang a calendar in some strategic location in their house to communicate information that affects the family, such as travel schedules, sports schedules, family celebrations, or doctors' appointments. Many people put their calendar on the refrigerator, since *everyone* ends up there sooner or later!

Special Events

If you enjoy many outings—concerts, lectures, sports events—but have difficulty keeping track of them, you may wish to keep a separate "Events Calendar." When you receive a notice of an upcoming event, list it on your events calendar. Be sure, of course, to put definite commitments on your master calendar. Another option is to have a folder labeled "Schedules" in which you put these notices, or hang them on the bulletin board. Then if you have a free evening, you can check the folder to see what options you have. This is particularly helpful if you have out-of-town guests, and you are assisting them in planning their schedules, or you want to entertain them.

Posted: $50 Reward

Calendars used the way I've described help eliminate not only the paper clutter in your home, but the mind clutter that comes from having to remember too many details and dates at one time.

Inside the front of my calendar you will find a note: "$50 Reward for Return." Once you have tried using a calendar in the way I've described, you too will offer a reward for its safe return. You'll find it's worth far more!

AUGUST
S M T W T F S
1 2 3 4 5 6
7 8 9 10 11 12 13
14 15 16 17 18 19 20
21 22 23 24 25 26 27
28 29 30 31

Wednesday July 6
1988 — Day 188 — 178 days to come

APPOINTMENTS	MEMORANDA
8:00 *Call school*	✔ *Call Travel Agent*
8:30	*Read Contract*
9:00 *Interview – May* ℗	*Heard from John?*
9:30	✔ *Pay Tuition*
10:00 *Ad Hoc Meeting*	*Make room reservation*
10:30 *Room 680*	*Write proposal*
11:00	✔ *Call Lois*
11:30	*250-1362*
12:00 *Lunch – Alfred*	*Renew driver's license*
12:30 *Club*	*Register for seminar*
1:00	*7/13 ? 387-8007*
1:30	*Call Flow*
2:00	
2:30	
3:00 *Staff meeting*	
3:30	
4:00	
4:30	
5:00 *Leave for car pool*	
5:30	
6:00	

EXPENSE RECORD		ENTERTAINMENT	
BREAKFAST		AUTO	
LUNCH			
DINNER		MISC	
HOTEL		*Xeroxing*	5.00
TIPS		*supplies*	2.50
FARES			
POSTAGE			
PHONE CALLS		TOTAL	

7:30 *Dinner at Phillips*
701 Main St.
321-6713

The page-a-day calendar
(see back of book for order form)

7

Your "To Do" List

MOST OF US have had the experience of sitting in a meeting, or trying to go to sleep at 1:00 AM, and suddenly remembering, "Oh, I never called my insurance company about the cracked windshield." Or, driving home from the hardware store, and realizing you forgot to get that extra housekey you have been needing for the past month. Such experiences are the basis for the proverbial piles of notes scratched on the back of empty envelopes, the corner of the newspaper, or on any scrap of paper that happens to be laying around. Many of the pieces of paper in the piles around the house are there to serve as a reminder for something we want to do at some point in the future—next week, or maybe not until we retire!

To-Do or Not To-Do

The purpose of the "To Do" list is to provide a *consistent* place to compile notes to yourself, and in so doing, to eliminate many pieces of paper from your life. Dorothy Sarnoff, chairman of Speech Dynamics, Inc., calls

Please Note: Notes Can Be Hazardous to Your Health.

it "A depository for your thoughts." Keep in mind that the "To Do" list is not designed for those tasks that need to be done at a specific time, but for those tasks you want to do, but have not yet determined when. For example, "Mail a birthday card to Aunt Sally" does not go in the "To Do" list, but in the calendar. However, a note to buy birthday cards could go on your "To Do" list.

The "To Do" list can take many forms. There are probably as many kinds of "To Do" lists as there are list-makers. Some people decry the whole idea, feeling that if they write something down they might absolve themselves from doing it! In fact, it is the first step to developing a goal-setting technique which is essential for effective life management.

Actually, the "To Do" list offers considerable creative scope. Even choosing your paper will take some decision making. And then there's the question of what to call your list. Switching from a weak infinitive "To Do" to a more emphatic "Do" may do the trick for you!

Of course, one of the major joys of a "To Do" list is crossing items off when they are completed. One client admitted that periodically he makes lists of things he's already done just so he can cross them off!

How To-Do It

People have different criteria for what they include in their list and how they include it. Some people just use key words like "Call Jerry," but what if you look at the list and can't remember why? Others add notes about the topic to be discussed and the phone number, so they don't have to look it up when it's time to call. There is also the ongoing debate on whether to separate at-home to-do's from work to-do's. Some people keep a running list, and when it gets messy or full, they start over.

Some people create coded symbols to record their progress on a task. For example, WCB for "will call back" (meaning they will call her), TCB for "to call back" (meaning, she will call back), or NA for "no answer."

A major decision regarding the "To Do" list is whether to carry it with you. The proponents of the "To Do" list on a yellow legal pad obviously find this difficult. So some people use a small spiral notebook, or even index cards they can stick in their pocket. Once again the "Post-It" notes make a handy "To Do" list when you need to put it in a "can't miss it" place—such as in the car, on the outside of your briefcase or purse, or on the bathroom mirror.

I use *The "To Do" Book,* a small looseleaf notebook divided into sections with a pocket inside the front and back cover. The advantage of a loose-leaf notebook is that you can add and delete pages easily. The "To Do" Book has standard size 3½" × 6½" pages that you can find at the corner drugstore. (See back of book for order form.) I prefer this size, because I can carry it with me. This is a major timesaver. If I discover I have an extra ten minutes before I need to get to an appointment, and I am near a shopping center, I can check the "Errands" sections and find one or two things I can accomplish in that time. If I find I am stuck in a traffic jam or waiting in a doctor's office, I can use the time to plan projects, make my "To Do" list for the next day, or write a quick thank-you note. (I always carry one or two pieces of note stationery in the back pocket.)

Of course there are other options. A friend of mine uses a bound notebook of lined paper which she divides into categories (about one-third page for each). On each line she writes the "To Do's" within that category. When it's done, she crosses it off the list in another color. Then she has a permanent record of her activities, which is very interesting and can be very useful, over the years. If you run out of space in a particular category, write "see page so-and-so" and continue the category.

One basic principle when organizing anything is to "put like items together." This same principle applies when organizing lists. Put items on a "To Do" list together based on the kind of activity required. For example, list together all phone calls, letters to write, and errands to run. If you are running errands, you do not need to be hassled by a list of phone calls you need to make. On the other hand, if you are trying to make a series of phone calls, you do not need a note to buy scotch tape.

What to Make a To-Do About

Your "To Do" book can be divided into numerous categories, depending on your specific needs. The following are some possibilities.

Phone Calls: Here you can list the names of people you wish to call, with the phone number beside them to speed up the process. You may find it helpful to use one page in this section for personal calls and another for business. If you need to make a phone call at a *specific* time, use your calendar—not your "To Do" list (or both—as a security measure).

Letters: This section also could be divided into personal and business.

Discuss: This section provides a place to accumulate information you wish to discuss with a particular person. Use one page, or section of one page, for each person in your life with whom you relate frequently: child, spouse, secretary, committee chair, etc. Use another page to list the questions you want to ask your doctor at your next appointment, another to list the items that you need to discuss with your mechanic the next time you take your car to the garage, or another to list the concerns you want to raise at the next parent-teacher conference at school.

Errands: Have you ever gone past the appliance repair shop wishing you had the number of the vacuum filter so you could pick it up on the way home instead of making an extra trip? The "To Do" Book has a pocket to put the drycleaning receipts, etc., so you'll be sure to have it. This section will save you many miles of errand running. Group errands together according to geographical area, or type of store. Most people keep their grocery list in the kitchen, but if you happen to be at work when you think of something that needs to go on the list, this is a great place to put it. Then when you are ready to go grocery shopping, you can combine both lists.

Books: This section will eliminate those torn, yellowed newspaper articles about books you have been meaning to purchase. Use this page to list books you want to borrow from the library (Note the Library of Congress number when you look it up the first time, so you don't have to look it up again if the book was already checked out.). Use another page in this section to list books you have loaned to friends.

Gifts: Remember the gift you found hidden under the bed after your daughter's birthday was over? Here's a place to list the gifts you have on hand, and where they are located if you are afraid you will forget! You can use another page in this section to make a note when you overhear your father saying he really would like to have a good pair of binoculars. You might even make a list of gift ideas for yourself, in case your kids ever ask!

Projects: Planning to redecorate your living room, or give a Superbowl party? Here is a place to collect all the ideas you have. Then as you actually begin the project, you can enter the various steps into your calendar as they need to be completed.

Restaurants: Here you can record names of restaurants you would like to try with addresses and phone numbers and business hours. You may even wish to add the name of the maitre'd. Group the restaurants together by geographical area. Then if you are meeting a friend or client downtown, you can easily check your list to see which restaurant would be fun and convenient. This system will eliminate all the pieces of paper with restaurant reviews you have been saving. It's also fun when a guest comes to town and says, "Let's go out tonight." It will take you no time to choose your restaurant.

Travel: This is a terrific place to put a standard packing list for travel. Then each time you plan a trip to a new city, create a special page such as "New York" where you can make notes about particular things you want to take with you, people you want to see or places you want to go while you are there, or information about car rentals, hotel reservations, etc. Finally, make a "Before Trip Checklist" to remind you about those last-minute "To Do's" such as checking the thermostat, turning off the coffeepot, making arrangements to feed the cat, and stopping the newspaper. Some frequent travelers make an "After Trip Checklist" to remind themselves of something they want to do differently on the next trip.

Thoughts: How many times have you read a quote that intrigued you, or had a brainstorm about how to solve a particular problem and said to yourself, "I'll have to give that some thought"? Here you can write those ideas down, and when you find yourself caught in rush hour traffic, or waiting in the banker's office with nothing to do, you can choose "Thought" and think it!

Goals: Research shows that less than 3% of the U.S. population put their goals in writing. It also shows that having written goals is high on the priority list of high achievers. Whether you are making New Year's resolutions, or designing a business plan, this section provides a convenient place to keep track of your goals and your progress. Then it will be easy to check it periodically to see if your life activities reflect what you said you wanted to do!

Birthdays: This is a good place to list those special birthdays of family members and friends. You may create a special section, or include it in "Numbers." From this list it will be easy to translate into your calendar the days you need to mail the cards, or to purchase the cards you need when you are running errands.

Numbers: Frequently the papers in our piles contain numbers we need to remember: access codes to the cash machine, the long-distance service, or the security system, social security numbers for other family members, school bus numbers, clothing sizes or table dimensions. One client puts small samples of her wallpaper, paint, fabric swatches, etc., in her "To Do" book.

Remember I said one of the objectives of this paper management system is to eliminate unnecessary pieces of paper? Try just these first four aspects of the system—the "To Sort" tray, the wastebasket, the calendar, and the "To Do" list—and see how many you can toss already.

8

Your Names and Numbers

IF YOU SUDDENLY decide to take a trip to San Francisco, it is unlikely that you will even remember that the telephone number of your favorite cousin is in one of the letters buried on the desk. Even if you do remember, what are the chances you will have the time to look for it? Remember Hemphill's Principle: "If you don't know you have it, or you can't find it, it is of no value to you!" Many of the pieces of paper floating around our homes are there because of an important telephone number, or one we are afraid might *become* important to us.

The White and the Yellow

In our personal lives telephone numbers can be divided into two basic categories: (1) Relatives and close friends with whom we always want to stay in contact regardless of where we live, and (2) neighbors, services, stores, schools, organizations or government agencies with whom we will no longer have contact if we move.

In other words, each of us needs a personal "white pages" and a personal "yellow pages." For many people who move frequently, it is essential to separate those two categories, so when they do move, it is easy to tear out the "Minneapolis" yellow pages and start "Denver."

The first step in designing a good system for addresses and telephone numbers is to determine whether you wish to separate your "white pages" and your "yellow pages" into two separate systems, or use one system. Your choice will be influenced to some extent by the volume of information you wish to keep. If you are one of the few whose life is relatively simple, a single system will probably be plenty, but if you have an active community life, a family, a career, or travel frequently, you may need more than one.

Choose Your Listing System

The next step is to decide on the system of listing you will use. Options include a Rolodex, a preprinted telephone and address book, a box of alphabetized index cards, a looseleaf notebook, or your personal computer. In making your decision, keep in mind how portable your system needs to be, or whether you plan duplicate systems for office, home (more than one floor?), vacation home, or travel. Whether you choose to use a Rolodex or a notebook, or some other system, the determining factor in the success of your system is ensuring that you will be able to retrieve the information when you need it.

You will probably need a complete listing of white and yellow pages at your work area. In addition, most people carry a small telephone book, or use the back of their calendar (for the most often used numbers from each system), which they can carry with them when they are away from home. If you use a separate small phone book, instead of the back of your calendar, you will not have to worry about rewriting the phone info at the end of each year. If your home has more than one floor, or if you have more than one home, you will need additional systems to accommodate those needs.

But How Can I Find It?

Do not assume that all information should be recorded in the same way. For example, sometimes you may list a number under the name of the individual, other times under the name of the company or organization, sometimes under the type of service they perform, and in rare instances, perhaps, even under the name of the person who introduced you. Sometimes you may wish to record numbers under more than one category. For example, you may have one card for Household Repairs on which you list several services. However, you may have a separate card for "Pipewrench, Peter—Plumber," or "Plumber—Peter

Pipewrench." As a general rule, however, the simpler the system is, the more inclined you will be to use it. Ask yourself the question, "If I wanted to contact this person, what word would I think of?" Use that answer as your key word.

The Rolodex

If you have never tried using a Rolodex, I strongly encourage you to do so, particularly for your "yellow pages." If you have any system that isn't working, start over. In purchasing a Rolodex, I recommend one with 3x5 size cards. They are large enough to staple or scotch tape business cards directly onto (that way you don't have to copy the information) and they are large enough to give you plenty of writing space. The smaller size may be just what you need beside the phone in your bedroom.

A standard format will make your Rolodex easier to use. Put the key word, that is the individual's name (last name first), organization, or service in the upper left hand corner, and the phone number in the upper right, as this is the information you will need most often. Under the key word, list the address.

In addition to name, address, and telephone number, the Rolodex card can be used for recording other useful information: key people, a simple record of correspondence or telephone exchanges, birthdays, anniversaries, dates of special events. It is also an excellent place for tracking your holiday card list. Make a small chart in the lower right hand corner with three columns—one for the year, one for "sent," and one for "received" where you can place checkmarks. Some people create a separate holiday list, but incorporating it into an existing system frequently means less work and fewer systems to keep updated.

There is no law which says that a Rolodex card can only be used for addresses and phone numbers. The Rolodex is a perfect place to record that crucial bit of information, such as the combination to your favorite padlock or social security numbers for your family. Think of it as a "mini-file" for odd bits of information.

Rolodex cards come in a variety of colors you can use to indicate different categories.

Emergency!

There is a serious side to all of this. If your child is violently ill from drinking a poisonous substance, you will not have time to sort through a pile of papers to find the emergency number for the poison control center.

Post a list of emergency numbers by at least one telephone on each floor. Include police, fire, poison control center, work numbers for family members and any neighbor or friend you might call in an emergency.

HEMPHILL, Barbara   (202)387-8007
Barbara Hemphill Associates
1718 Connecticut Avenue
Suite 410
Washington, D.C. 20009

(In this space you could note date/subject of telephone calls, directions to get to the office, etc.)

HOUSE REPAIRS

Plumber—Peter Pipewrench	222-4387
Electrician—Henry Wire	425-3098
Painter—Betty Brush	620-4487

SOCIAL SECURITY NUMBERS

Barbara	508-60-3827
Alfred	312-59-8887
Jenny	508-69-1111
Thoma	508-29-8034

COMBINATION LOCKS

| 16-3-5 | (GYM) |
| 15-1-7 | (BICYCLE) |

Sample Rolodex Cards

9

Your Action Files

AFTER YOU HAVE eliminated as many pieces of paper as possible by using your wastebasket calendar, your "To Do" list, and your telephone listing, the remaining papers will fall into one of two categories:

1. *Action Files.* Action files are for those papers that need your attention immediately, or at some point in the near future (as opposed to the "some day" projects).
2. *Reference Files.* Reference files are for those pieces of paper you know you will, or think you might need, at some point in the future.

The system is particularly effective if you keep two points in mind:

1. *A Reference File can become an Action File or vice versa.* For example, a Reference File called "Entertaining" can become an Action File if you are planning a party. When the party is over, that Action File returns to the Reference Files. (Be sure to take a few minutes to throw out any excess papers at this point, instead of saying, "I've got to clean that file out someday." It

is much quicker and easier to do while the information is fresh in your mind).

2. *You can have an Action File and a Reference File with the same or similar file headings.* For example, you might have a Reference File entitled "Community Association" and an Action File entitled "Community Association—Dues Campaign."

When Action is Too Packed

Clients with great piles of paper on their desks will frequently say, "I need all of this on my desk because I am working on it." But often a close look will determine that, even though all the papers on the desk may need to be saved (although not as often as they think!), not all of them are necessary to complete the particular project. A bulky Action File often indicates that some of those papers could go in a Reference File, or you may have two Action Files for one project, such as "Party—Menus" and "Party—Invitations."

If you lead a very simple lifestyle, you may find that one file called "Action" is all you need, but for

many people a pile of papers that need action would soon topple over! When the pile gets that deep, it is difficult to do anything. It soon takes as much time to find a project as it does to do it! When that situation exists, a major issue is decision-making.

The Next Step

Remember that clutter is symptomatic of postponed decisions. To simplify the decision-making process, it is helpful to recognize that the papers we need to take action on fall into categories. To determine the category into which a particular piece of paper falls, ask yourself the question, "What is the *next* action I need to take on this piece of paper?" The answer will tell you into which Action File to put the paper. There are several possible answers to the question, and each answer is an Action File category.

The following are potential Action File categories:

Call
Calls Waiting
Discuss
File
Hold for Future
Pay
Projects (one for each, e.g., "Remodeling")
Read
Take to Office/Home
Write (Could divide into personal/business)
Upcoming Meetings/Trips (One for each, e.g., "New York")
Xerox

It is crucial that you recognize the significance of the word *next* in the question, "What is the *next* required action on this piece of paper?" Sometimes it takes time to find the answer. Your initial reaction may be, "I have to call Joe," but then you realize you want to call Nancy first. Then you realize you can't talk intelligently to Nancy until you have read a particular document. So finally, the answer may be to make an appointment with yourself (noted in your calendar) to "Read Bylaws" with a symbol Ⓒ to remind you that the information you need to discuss with Nancy related to that issue is in "Call."

Let us take a look at each of the potential categories for Action Files to see how they could be used.

Call—Many times the next action required on a piece of paper is a telephone call to someone. In addition to putting the paper in the "Call" file, you may wish to make a note on your calendar on the day you need to make the call. Using a symbol such as Ⓒ will remind you that there is additional information in the "Call" file.

Calls Waiting—How many times have you received a telephone call in which the conversation began, "Hello. This is Anne Smith. I am returning your call."? The knot in the pit of your stomach tightens, as you frantically try to remember why you called her, or even who she is! If you have a note in your "Calls Waiting" file that tells you why you have left a message for that person to return your call, it can be a real stress-saver. In addition, you can check the file periodically to check the current status of the calls. Were you simply returning their call, and the ball is now in their court, or do you really want to talk to them? If the former, after a period of time, throw the paper out. If the latter, take the paper out of "Calls Waiting" and put it in "Call," with a note on your calendar to make the call again.

Discuss—Communication is a major factor in managing the paper in our lives. Frequently we cannot take action on a matter until we have discussed it with another person. All of us have certain people in our lives with whom we routinely discuss issues, whether it is a spouse, a child, a colleague or friend, or a professional resource. The "Discuss" category will contain several subcategories. For example, "Discuss—Mary", "Discuss—Accountant."

File—Most people dislike filing and will put it off as long as possible. Even if you don't mind filing, but the file cabinet is in another room, you will need a "File" for those pieces of paper that need to go into the Reference Files. Many of the pieces of paper that arrive in the mail can go directly into "File" and never clutter the top of your desk. (For more complete information, see Chapter 10.)

Hold for Future—Many names have been applied to this category—suspension, suspense, tickler, or pending are some examples. This is not a place to put papers that require action from you at this time. Rather, it is for papers that will require action at some future date, or that will require action after you have received additional information. When you are tempted to put a piece of paper in this category because you are not certain of your decision, ask yourself, *"What am I going to know tomorrow that I don't know today?"* If the answer is "Nothing," you will know that you need to look further into the issue to find out what other category the paper really belongs in. If you simply cannot make a decision at this time, and you want to postpone the decision, put the paper in "Hold," but make a note on your calendar to remind you to consider the issue again. If you receive an invitation to dinner and with the invitation are the directions for getting to the host's home, put the invitation in "Hold for Future" with a symbol such as Ⓗ beside the engagement notation on your calendar.

Pay—This is the category to put all the bills you need to pay, as well as any other paper that requires writing a check—an order you wish to place, or a donation you would like to make. If your household finances are quite complicated, you may wish to subdivide this category. For example, you could have a "Must Pay" for mortgage, utilities, and car payment and a "Would Like to Pay" for potential donations, orders, magazine subscriptions. If you pay some of the bills, and your spouse pays others, you may wish to subdivide the category into "Pay—Betty" and "Pay—Bill." This is also a good place to put payment coupon books and reminders of deductions that are taken from your checking account automatically.

Projects—Each project should have a separate file. Those that are currently active fall into the Action File category, while those that are completed, or have been put "on hold" temporarily, go into the Reference File category. If the project involves many papers, it may be appropriate to have a Reference File and an Action File for that project. The Action File would contain only those papers you need to complete the current step of the project. When that step is completed, those papers would go into the Reference File and the papers relating to the next step of the project would be filed in the Action File. Project Files should be arranged alphabetically.

Take To Office/Home—Be sure to designate a particular place to put those papers (and other items) you need to take with you to work. Choose a convenient location—near the door or put them straight into your briefcase. Then choose a place to call "Home" for your briefcase, so you can always find it when you need to put something there. If you do have something you want to put in your briefcase, but you cannot find it, put the item where your briefcase *should* be. Then when

you find the briefcase, it will be easy to get them together. This will stop the frustrating game of having
one and not the other, and vice versa.

Write—Many times the next action you need to take
on a piece of paper is writing a letter. "Write" includes business letters, personal letters, thank you
notes, and special occasion cards.

If this is a problem area for you, take some time
thinking about what you can do to make the task easier. Many people find it helps to physically separate
these categories. Sometimes you may feel like spending ten minutes writing a thank you note, but not an
hour writing an old college roommate. If you have to
dig through a huge pile to find what interests you at
the moment, you may lose interest before you find it!

I use airport waiting time to look for greeting cards
I like. I keep a supply of favorites on hand, so sending a congratulations card literally takes only minutes—and I'm sure doing it makes me feel every bit
as good as the person to whom I sent it!

Keep postcards on hand for quick notes. Many people are now writing responses on the bottom of business letters and returning them to the sender to speed
up response time. If you need a copy, put the paper
in "Xerox" or "Take to Office" or use carbon or copyset
paper.

If you are procrastinating about writing a letter, ask
yourself if a phone call would suffice, or at least get
the process started. Or, write an outline for yourself
to help organize your thoughts and make the letter
less difficult to write.

Upcoming Meetings/Trips—Virtually every time you
plan to go to a meeting or take a trip, you will accumulate papers related to that event, whether it is an
airplane ticket, a meeting agenda, or a note from a

friend asking you to call or visit when you are in the city.

When the trip or meeting is over, throw away those pieces of paper that are no longer essential, and file the remaining papers away according to how you will use them next. For example, the letter from your friend might contain an address that could be entered in your phone listing, and then the letter could be tossed. Or you may wish to put the letter in your "Mementos" box to read again in the years to come. (See Chapter 15.)

Xerox—Many times you cannot take the next action on a piece of paper until you get a xerox copy. Such is frequently the case in submitting medical insurance claims. Or, you want to send a clipping from the local newspaper to your sister, but you also want a copy for yourself. (This is also a good place to keep coupons from your local copy center.)

The major advantage to this system is an increased ability to manage your time effectively. It is a good time management practice to group like activities together. Then, when you have ten minutes before you need to meet your child at school, a quick look in "Call" can help you use those ten minutes to your advantage. If you are going to an appointment where you may have to wait, take along "Write" with some stationery for personal notes or some scratch paper to draft more formal correspondence. If you have finally corralled your spouse long enough to get some of the family bills paid, but then can't find the bills, your stress level skyrockets.

Logistics Strategy

You may well be feeling quite overwhelmed at this point! Anything new can seem overwhelming, so don't despair too early in the game. One question you may have is "Where do I put all these files?" Start with a series of manila file folders. You can put them in the front of the filing drawer in your desk, if there is one, or in a stand-up rack on top of your desk, or in a series of stack trays on your desk. Some people, who are afraid of the "out of sight out of mind" trap, use a series of categorized piles on or near their desk.

As you experiment with the system, you will discover that each category does not have to be a "file" per se, nor does it have to be on your desk. For example, I know of no one whose "Read" category will fit into a file folder, and most people don't read at their work area. So "Read" could be in a basket beside your easy chair, the bed, or even in the bathroom! (Or, most likely, a combination.) (See Chapter 16 for more detailed information on "Read.") You may want to keep "Xerox" in a folder near the door or in your briefcase so you will have it when you go out.

All Those Files!

Another question you may have is "How do I remember to look in all those files?" Try it! You can put a symbol on your calendar to remind you to look. In many instances, such as "Call," there will undoubtedly be one call you will automatically remember to make. When you check the file for information on that call, you will be reminded of the others you want to make.

You may be confused with the similarity of the categories for the "To Do" list (Chapter 7) and the Action Files. Sometimes your "To Do" is just a thought, in which case you write it in your "To Do" book (or on a piece of paper in your Action File). Other times, the "To Do" involves a piece of paper that goes in the Action File. It is not a duplication, unless you choose to use a duplication system as an insurance policy.

You may not want or need all of the Action File categories I have described. If the entire idea seems overwhelming to you, choose a few that appeal to you most, and try them. If you're anything like the hundreds of people who have adopted the system to their own lifestyles, you'll soon *love* it and wonder how you ever managed without it.

10

Reference Files

THE REASON FOR creating Reference Files is not just to be able to put papers away, but to be able to find them again! Research shows that 80% of the papers in most files are never used. So before you even begin to think about where you should file any piece of paper, think seriously about whether you should file it at all!

If you have a filing system that is not working, or if you inherited someone else's system, start over. Then incorporate the information from the old system into the new system as you need it.

There are three components of an effective Reference File:

1. Management
2. Mechanics
3. Maintenance

Frequently, in my work with clients, I discover that two of these three factors are already in operation. As soon as the third factor is taken into account, the system starts to work.

File Management

After you have considered the other five possibilities for a piece of paper—Wastebasket, Calendar, "To Do" list, Rolodex/Phone Book, and Action files—and have determined that you wish to save this information for future use in the Reference Files, you need to decide how you will find it when you want it.

Fear of Filing

One of the reasons people resist filing papers away is a fear that they will make a poor decision and file the paper in an inappropriate or hard-to-remember file. Here are some guidelines that will help you with your filing decisions:

1. *Ask yourself, "Under what circumstances would I want this information?"* Be specific! "Just in case" will not help you find it again! If the answer is, "I might want this information if I were writing a speech," then "Speech Ideas" is a good location. If you answer, "I will need this when I sell the house," then "House—Main Street" might be the answer.

2. *Ask yourself, "If I wanted this information, what word would first enter my mind?"* The answer to that question will tell you what Reference File is appropriate for this piece of paper. For example, a flyer about ordering candy from a specialty company could be filed under "Gift Ideas" or "Mail Order Info." And invitations from a past party could be filed under "Party Ideas," "Printing Ideas," or "Mementos."

3. *File information according to how you will use it, not where you got it.* For example, your local homeowner's association published an article recommending repair services in the area. Suppose you wake up one morning to discover that you have no hot water for a

shower. What are the chances you would remember that article in the "Homeowner's Association" file? A file labeled "Services—Household Repair" might be more useful.

4. *Put all papers in their most general category first, such as "Warranties and Instructions."* Then, if the file becomes too bulky, break it down into "Warranties and Instructions—Appliances," "Warranties and Instructions—Clothing," etc.

It is easier to look through one file with twenty pieces of paper, than ten files with two papers in each: fewer places to look, fewer places to lose. The added advantage is that, when you are using a file to get a particular piece of paper you remember, you will also discover other pieces of paper you have forgotten. As a result, you will be able to use more of the information you file.

5. *If a paper could be filed in two places, choose the one you are most likely to look in first.* Write a note on the second file folder which says, "See also. . . ." If you feel it is essential, you can make a copy for the second file.

6. *Organize your files consistently.* For example, you may have medical and educational records for several members of the family. Decide whether you want all of John's files together; i.e., "John—Education," "John—Medical," or do you want all medical files together, i.e., "Medical—Ann," "Medical—John."

File Index

A file index is the final, and perhaps the most important step in managing your files. The same information can be filed several ways. For example, I could file information about my car in "Automobile," "Car," "Chrysler," or "Vehicle." The problem comes if you file it under "Car" one time, and under "Chrysler" the next—and your spouse looks for it under "Automobile!" This dilemma can be avoided by making an alphabetical list of the file names. When you are writing or typing the index, leave space between each letter of the alphabet so you will have room to add new file titles as you need them. Put as many names on one page as possible. It is unlikely you will ever get to the filing if you have to read a 15-page guide first!

Keep your file index accessible in the very front of your filing system, or at your desk. When you are reading an article you want to file, check the index to see what file already exists which might be appropriate for that particular article.

Use the index if you are looking for an article. It is much easier to check a file index to see where you might find an article than it is to open the file drawer and go through file after file.

The index is particularly important if you are learning a new system, or if more than one person will be using the same system. Keep in mind also that if there is a particular piece of paper you are afraid of losing, you can list it on the index. For example, "Birth Certificate"—See "Legal Information."

Sample Headings for Your System

The following is a list of the kinds of information that can be put in a home filing system. They are listed here alphabetically. However, you may wish to put them into various categories. A friend of mine divides her files into three categories: Financial and legal, reference, and children. Some people put all files that involve payments of any kind into one category, and all other files in a reference category. Be aware that there are always gray areas when you begin categorizing. For example, you might think of "Medical" as a reference file or a financial file. You can eliminate the problem of determining what category a file should be in by filing everything strictly by the alphabet. Then, if you are looking for "Medical," there is no question of where to look.

Keep in mind also that your filing system will change when your life circumstances change. For example, if you get married, you will need to decide whether to maintain two separate filing systems or combine them into one. If you decide to combine them, you may want to use color to identify files which belong specifically to one person.

ART OWNED (Could be under Personal Property or Insurance)

ARTICLES (This could be divided into categories by subject; e.g. "Articles—Psychology")

BOOK INFORMATION (This could be divided into categories: Books—Novels; Books—History)

CAR MAINTENANCE or Automobile or Volvo

CHILDCARE INFORMATION (or Babysitter) (Include summer camp information and photocopies of blank forms to be filled out with information for the sitter)

CHRISTMAS (Ideas for gifts, copies of annual letter, record of gifts given, ideas for next year)

CHURCH (This could be listed under specific name: Calvary Presbyterian Church, for example)

CONSUMER INFORMATION (This can be divided into categories if it becomes too bulky)

CREDIT CARDS (Enter card number, address, and phone number to call if card is lost; put duplicate copies of card)

DEATH INFORMATION (What to do in case of your death or a relative's; copy of wills)

DIET INFORMATION (This could also be placed under Health or Nutrition)

ENTERTAINMENT (Put ideas for outings for family or houseguests. This could be divided into categories.)

EDUCATION RECORDS (Make one file for each member of family: include information about school)

FINANCIAL RECORDS (Separate general financial planning info from your personal information. This could contain information about loans, mortgages, etc.)

GARDENING AND PLANTS

GIFT IDEAS

HOBBIES (Divide into specific areas such as Stamps, Coins)

HOME DECORATING (Divide into specific areas if too bulky for one file)

HOUSEHOLD MAINTENANCE RECORDS

HUMOR (Favorite cartoons, jokes, articles)

INCOME TAX INFORMATION (divided into years) (Records of donations, taxes paid, receipts for any tax deductible item)

INSURANCE—Car

INSURANCE—Household/Personal Property (include receipts for art, jewelry, furs, etc.)

INSURANCE—Life

INSURANCE—Medical (use 3 folders:
Bills To Be Submitted—Include blank forms
Bills Submitted But Not Paid
Bills Paid)

INVENTORY (List items in various storage areas of your home or in other locations)

IRA (Could be included in "Retirement Information")

MAPS & INSTRUCTIONS (Directions to friend's homes; photocopies of map to your home)

PARTY RECORDS (Guest lists, menus of past parties, ideas for future)

PERSONAL PROPERTY (Specifics on valuable items owned, if not already in Insurance file)

QUOTES & FAVORITE ARTICLES (or Speech Ideas if you make frequent public appearances)

RECREATION (can be divided into various sports)

RESTAURANTS (reviews, menus)

RESUME INFORMATION

RETIREMENT INFORMATION

SAFE DEPOSIT BOX (Keep a list of what is located there)

SERVICES (Could be divided into "Personal" and "Household")

SHOPPING INFORMATION (Mail order info; clippings about new stores, brochures)

SPECIAL INTERESTS (Divide into categories such as "Psychology")

SUBSCRIPTIONS & MEMBERSHIPS (Records of renewals, order forms)

STOCK INFORMATION (Can be divided into name of stock)

TRAVEL (Divide into geographic areas, depending on quantity)

WARRANTIES AND INSTRUCTIONS (Divide into types; e.g., "Major Appliances.")

You will probably not use all of these categories, and you may have others. One client has a file labeled "Warm Fuzzies" for those days she really needs a boost!

Safe Deposit Boxes

Adoption, birth, death, or marriage certificates; car titles; deeds to property; military papers; stock certificates, or other papers that are difficult or impossible to replace should be kept in a safe deposit box. However you might want to place a note in the appropriate file to remind you where the particular document is. (See Chapter 10.)

File Mechanics

The importance of the mechanics of a filing system is frequently overlooked. Very few people enjoy filing; most people dislike it intensely! There are two major reasons: (1) They dislike deciding where to file the papers, and (2) they dislike the physical discomfort of jamming hands into overstuffed file drawers, or looking into numerous file drawers before they find the file they are looking for.

Your Choice of File Cabinet

Choosing your file cabinet is an important decision. My first choice, without a doubt, is a good-quality full suspension file cabinet. "Full suspension" means that you can open the drawers all the way, so that no files are obstructed from easy view. For most households, a two-drawer vertical cabinet will be enough. These cabinets are generally 28" high, 15" wide and 26" deep. The drawer pulls out the full depth of the cabinet, and files are arranged from front to back. If you want or need more filing space, you can purchase a three-, four-, or five-drawer vertical file.

If you want to create additional working space in your work area, a good choice would be a two-drawer full suspension lateral file cabinet. These are generally 28" high, 18" deep and come in widths of 30", 36" or 42". The depth is approximately 35" when the drawer is open, and the files can be arranged front to back in rows, or side to side. Any good office supply store will have a catalog in which you can see pictures of the various options, even if they do not have them in stock.

You can find less expensive file cabinets at a discount store, but I do not recommend them for files you use frequently. If you cannot afford a full suspension file, you may find that filing boxes are more accessible than a poorly made metal cabinet. Keep in mind that a good quality file cabinet is a lifetime investment. Prices vary dramatically, so after you have found the cabinet you want, compare prices.

Decide whether to purchase letter or legal size files. Unless your life is complicated with many legal issues and you have a substantial amount of legal-sized paper, I would recommend letter size. You will take up less space and save a significant amount of money on the cost of the file cabinet and the file folders.

If you do not have room for a traditional filing cabinet, or you feel it does not fit with your interior decor, there are other options ranging from a cardboard or plastic file box to solid wood cabinets designed to match your furniture. Portable file folders work well if you use your kitchen or dining room table as a workspace, and want to move the files with you when you work. They also work well for files which you access only occasionally, and which you store in the basement, attic, garage or some other out-of-the-way place.

Your Choice of File Folders

One of the major decisions to make in setting up a filing system is what kind of file folders you will use. There are multiple options.

"Hanging Files" (Pendaflex) are my preference. Although they are more expensive than manila folders, they will last significantly longer, and the plastic stand-up tabs make the labels much easier to read.

If your filing cabinet does not accommodate hanging files, you can purchase a hanging file (Pendaflex) frame which can be sized to fit your file drawer.

It is not necessary to put manila files inside the hanging files, unless you take the file out of the folder to use it. For example, a file for a committee on which you serve will need a manila folder so you can take it with you to the meeting. Frequently, however, you just take out the paper from the file and the hanging file is sufficient. If you do use two folders, label the hanging file and the manila file identically. This will make it easy to return the file to its proper place.

In some cases, you use manila files to make subdivisions in a file. For example, the hanging folder could be labeled "Car", and the manila folders labeled "Car Insurance", "Car Repairs", etc. There are special files, called "Interior Files" which are slightly shorter than regular manila files, so there is no risk of the tabs obstructing the view of the plastic tabs.

Pendaflex also makes Box Bottom files which are useful for very thick files, or a file with many subdivisions. These have a one to three-inch cardboard strip in the bottom. If you are using manila files, creasing the fold lines at the bottom of the folder will increase the capacity of the folder, and prevent obstruction of the file label.

Hanging folders come in a variety of colors, as do other types of file folders. The hanging folders sometimes come with colored plastic tabs, but in the case of the darker colors such as red and blue, you may prefer to substitute clear plastic labels which are easier to read, particularly if you used typed labels.

Plastic tabs can go on the front or back of hanging

files. Most people prefer the back, because it is consistent with the label on the back of manila folders. The big advantage of putting the label on the front is that when you are filing a piece of paper, and you grab the plastic tab, the file will automatically open to the place you need to file the paper. Use whichever method you prefer, but be consistent.

There are also many other kinds of file folders available. If you have no filing cabinet, but have shelf space, you may want to use file folders with labels on the narrow end, instead of on the top. Then you can put your files on shelves, and still see the labels easily.

Some people like to use file folders with metal fasteners so that the papers can be punched and put in the file in chronological order, knowing they will stay that way. In most instances, I find that the results are not worth the effort. Over and over again, I have seen filing pile up because it took too much time and effort to get the holes punched.

Able Labels

Labeling is the key to an effective filing system. Often I find files with penciled labels, or no label at all, because they are only "temporary" files. But many become like the "temporary" building on my college campus which served as the music building for 27 years! It is very simple to buy a box of peel-off file labels, so that if you need to change the label, you can do so in a minute. In the meantime, you have a file you can easily read.

Determine what the label should say by asking the question, *"If I wanted this information again, what word would I think of?"* as previously discussed in "File Management."

Type labels only if a typewriter is always available, and you are comfortable enough with the typewriter to be able to do it easily, or have someone do it for you. Even though I am a proficient typist, and have a secretary, I still prefer to handwrite file labels, because they are easier to read. Use a dark-colored felt-tipped pen of medium thickness. One client attaches a pen on a string inside the file cabinet so it is always there when she wants it! I find printing labels in capital letters creates the most consistent, readable appearance.

Avoid using multiple colors, unless you use the color to identify certain files. Color is very useful if it tells a story, but very confusing if it doesn't. For example, you could use red labels on any files that contain information you will need at tax time, or use a different color for each member of the family. There are many ways to color code your files—colored file folders, colored file labels, colored dots to stick on labels, or colored pens to write labels. However, I would caution you to use color sparingly, unless you have someone to help you with the file mechanics, or you particularly enjoy doing it yourself. It can be very frustrating when you want to make a file quickly, and you can't find the right color label, pen or dot. Beware of the "Just for now" trap! Keep the system simple enough that you can maintain it as you go.

Put the key word at the left of the label when writing or typing labels. For example, "Education—John—1987" rather than "1987—Education—John."

Too Many Systems

One of the temptations, and most frequent mistakes, in setting up a filing system is to create too many systems. In doing this, you create more work for yourself. If you are looking for information, you first have to remember which filing system it is in, and then where it is in the system. If you are trying to file information, you may find it difficult to determine which system is appropriate for that information. Unless there is a clear-cut identity, such as all files involving financial information, keep all files together in one A-Z system. Then if you are looking for "Entertaining," you will go directly to "E", instead of wondering whether you put it in the "personal" files or the "house" files.

Special Mechanics Tips

The following are additional tips that will make the mechanics of your filing easier:

1. *Avoid using paper clips in files whenever possible.* They take up more space, and more importantly, catch on papers when you file them, obstructing the file label. Keep a staple remover handy, and staple papers together that are related.

2. *File papers with the most recent on the top.* When you open the file you can immediately see the latest action or information. This will also make cleaning the file take less time, because the oldest information will automatically be on the bottom.

3. *Arrange the file folders alphabetically.* If you have resisted this idea in the past, try it. You will be surprised at how much more quickly you will be able to find the file you are looking for.

4. *Label the outside of the file cabinet as to its contents, either by subject or by alphabet.* This will save you opening the third drawer when the file you want is in the second.

File Maintenance

No matter how much time and energy you spend creating a system to fit your particular needs, you will still need to adopt a plan to maintain the system. The following steps will help.

1. Determine when—or if—you will do the filing. More and more professional people are recognizing that it is cost effective to hire someone else to do the routine household management tasks—including filing—just as we hire others to maintain the lawn.

If you will be doing the work yourself, decide how you will keep the "File" pile from becoming larger than the file cabinet. Some people file when they pay bills. That way, two potentially unpleasant tasks are done at the same time, and you can reward yourself with a more pleasant activity when you are finished. Other people wait until the "File" tray is full.

Remember that if you circle the key word, or write it in the upper right hand corner, the filing task will be only a mechanical one and will take only minutes. The major reason people procrastinate about filing is that they don't like making the decision about where the paper should be filed. That decision is easier to make when you have just read the letter or article. This method is essential if someone else does your filing, because no two people would necessarily put a paper in the same file. A paper relating to your car insurance, for example, could be filed under "Car" or "Insurance." In this instance, the File Index again becomes invaluable.

2. Clean out the files as you use them. I cannot count how many dozens of times I have seen a client with a paper in hand they knew could be tossed say, "I'll have to clean this out someday," and promptly put the piece of paper back into the file again, instead of directly into the wastebasket!

3. *Establish an annual "File Clean Out Day"*—around tax time is frequently a good time, since you will be looking into files at that time anyway. An alternative is to wait until you need the file space. As long as you have room to file papers easily, the issue of purging is not a major one. But when you neglect filing the paper you would like to file, because it is physically uncomfortable or downright impossible to get your fingers into the file cabinet, then the time for Clean Out Day has arrived!

How Long is Enough?

Determine how long you need to keep the papers you file. Date information when you file it, so it will be easy to tell if it is recent enough to be useful. In certain cases, such as a file of newsletters, you can put the retention information right on the file label. For example, "Community Newsletter—Keep 1 year."

The issue of retention guidelines is a difficult one, particularly with regard to papers involving money transactions. However, I have seen dozens of people refuse to make any decisions about retention, because they are certain there is a "right" answer, and as soon as they discover what that is, they will begin to purge. There is no such answer. If you compare five authorities on records retention guidelines, you may get three different answers. The only person who can make that decision is you.

How do you do that? First of all, consult the person who assists you in preparing your tax returns. Check your local library to see if they have any guidelines which will help you. There are also guidelines in the

Appendix at the end of the book that will help you decide what is appropriate for you.

There are other factors to consider in making your decision. One is space. If you have enough space (say a basement) to keep everything, and it doesn't make you feel uncomfortable to have that paper lying around, then ignore it. Be careful, however, to separate the "archival materials" from those you are currently using. But if you get a knot in your stomach every time you open the file drawer or closet door, then the price you are paying for your failure to make decisions about paper retention is high, and you should look for alternatives.

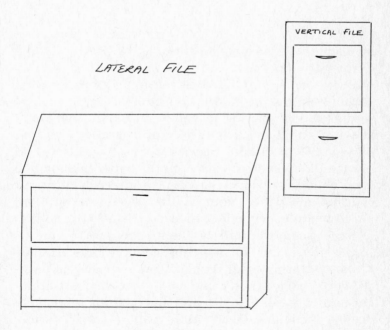

11

Strategies for Paper Management

EVERY PIECE OF paper in your life can be managed by using the techniques described in the previous seven chapters.

However, there are several categories of papers that particularly plague many households. There are essential papers relating to paying taxes and bills, and keeping family records. There are photographs and other family mementos, recipes, books, magazines, and newspapers. There is the issue of papers relating to your children—papers you need to keep about your children and papers your children need to keep relating to the management of their own lives. Other kinds of paper seem to multiply like mushrooms in various places around the house—maps, coupons, ads for some services which appear regularly on your doorstep, instruction books that come with new kitchen appliances and garden tools, and flyers from local businesses. Activities create more paper—travel, family celebrations, seminars, recreation and sports events. Medical emergencies, educational pursuits, career changes, job responsibilities, religious affiliations, club memberships, and community involvement create even more paper.

You will undoubtedly have questions about certain pieces of paper and will discover a variety of ways you could handle them. How do you know which is best?

No Right or Wrong Way

Remember, there is no "right" or "wrong" way to organize anything. If you asked three different interior designers to decorate your living room, you would obviously get three different results. You might like all three of them, but probably one of them would appeal to you more than the others. If you asked three different people to write a newspaper article about a community event, you would undoubtedly get three different stories. They would probably all be accurate but would be colored by the personal experiences and views of the individual authors.

Paper management has this same variety and flexibility. The next ten chapters will discuss some of the major areas of paper management that you will have to face in your life. You will find different approaches for handling these challenges, along with some of the pros and cons for each method. Choose the way that sounds the most feasible to you. Be sure to give it a fair try. Many people fail in setting up new systems because they do not allow enough time to develop the new habits, which is necessary to make any kind of change in their life. Try the new system for a reasonable amount of time. The amount of time required will be different for each individual, but two to three months is usually adequate. If the new system is still not working, ask yourself these three questions: (1) "Is the problem that I don't have enough time? If so, what can I do to make the time?" (2) "Am I having problems with the mechanics? If so, who can help me?" (3) "Do I really want to do this? If not, is there anyone else who can do it? Or, what would happen if I didn't do it? What would I do then?"

Most likely, all that will be required for success is a modification of the system. Spend some time identifying what you liked about the system you tried and what you did not. With that information, you can move on to make the necessary changes to create a system that will work for you.

Who's in Charge Here?

One of the questions that inevitably arises in every household is *who* is going to manage the paper? Answering this question can create a major conflict if there is no one in the family who is willing to do it, or if there is a disagreement about how the paper should be handled.

Communication and negotiation are the keys to success in family paper management. In most households, specific responsibilities are assigned to specific people. One person may pay bills, while another does the filing. Or, a husband and wife may elect to pick a "bill paying night" and do it together. In terms of filing, it is important that, even if one person generally does the filing, the other family members know something about the system in case that person is ill or absent. If one person tears out an article from a newspaper to be filed, that same person should identify where to file it if he or she expects to be able to find it again. (See Chapter 10 for more details on this subject.) In fact, every member of the household will have some papers to handle. Children need to learn to take care of their own papers if they are to become independent, psychologically healthy human beings.

If one member of the family has more skill in paper management, or more willingness to learn, the entire family will undoubtedly benefit. In that case, the paper manager of the family should be given special consideration in other household management areas such as shopping, errands, household maintenance, or outdoor maintenance.

As it is with any attempt at learning something new, you will discover stumbling blocks. Don't let that stop you! In every organizing process, things will seem worse before they get better. This is not the time to stop for a cup of coffee! A natural outcome of sorting through piles of papers is a renewed awareness that we are not as productive as we would like to be. Concentrate on how you are going to improve the situation now, not what you should have done in the past.

How Does it Make You Feel?

Sometimes my clients have a great deal of difficulty letting go of the excess in their lives, whether it is paper, clothes, kitchen utensils, or their children's outgrown toys. If that is true in your case, ask the question, "How does having this make me feel?" If the answer is anything negative—sad, angry, guilty— then decide whether you want to continue to surround yourself with anything that makes you feel unhappy.

Another factor that is very important is our ability to make decisions about what we need to keep is the clarity of our goals and our willingness to look to the future instead of dwelling on the past. If you find yourself unable to make progress with letting go of things you know deep down inside you really don't need, it might be one symptom of a deeper underlying problem. You may even wish to seek professional help in setting some specific goals for your life.

12

Bills, Bills, Bills

ONE OF THE inevitable facts of life is bills. We are able to laugh about many of the papers in our lives, but there is little humor in unpaid bills! Many of our papers will be forgotten if we ignore them long enough, but bills demand to be found. A lost bill can mean a disconnected telephone or a cold house in December. Bills often represent emotionally charged issues like the extravagant new suit that you've never worn or the vacation that fizzled.

With those unwelcomed bills come a bundle of questions. Not only must we deal with the issue of finding the money to pay bills, but there are issues of who pays them—when, where, and how. Frequently clients spend more time debating whether to postpone paying a bill than it would have taken to write the check. And how embarrassing it is when the mortgage company calls about your delinquent payment, and you can't even find the payment book!

Disorganized Bills

Organized Bills

It Pays To Keep Track of Your Bills.

Keeping Track

One of the major factors in reducing the stress of paying bills is establishing a method of keeping track of them. The simplest method, although not necessarily the most effective from a financial planning standpoint, is to simply put all the bills in one place. Sit down and pay them at least once a month, and then file all the receipts in one place, or in different places, depending on what the expense related to. If you need to refer to the payment, you will be able to find the information.

Note that it is not necessary to open a bill at the time you receive it, and *unless* you plan to do something specific with the information in the bill at that time, I don't particularly recommend it. The result of opening many bills is a significant increase in the number of pieces of paper you have to handle, and the likelihood that the bill and the envelope for returning your payment will get separated.

One method of keeping track of when to pay bills is to open them, and then mark the amount due and the due date on the front of the envelope. Then put a note in your calendar on the day you need to pay the bill. Another method is to make a list of the bills as they come in. Then you can check them off as you pay them, with the date paid and the check number. This can be useful for future reference.

Many people use, and most people think they ought to use, some kind of a budget book. This book is not intended to be a financial planning guide, as there are other good resources on that subject at your local bookstore or library. The issue as it relates to paper management, however, has to do with when you will use whatever book you choose. Decide whether you will enter the information in your budget book at the same time you pay bills or whether that is an unrealistic expectation for one sitting. If so, you will need to determine when you will fill out your budget book, just as you determined when you would pay your bills. Make an appointment with yourself and mark it in your calendar until it becomes a reliable habit.

A Time to Pay Up

The first step in creating a bill paying system that works for you is recognizing that it must be done—by someone. If you find it an abhorrent task, do not assume that *you* have to be that someone. More and more private individuals are hiring people to do tasks that can be delegated in order to allow themselves time and energy for other activities that are more fun, and may be profitable, thus providing funds to pay for the service. Inquire at the banks in your area to see if any offer a billpayer system that allows you to pay your bills by punching the amounts into your touchtone telephone.

If, however, you do not have the luxury of a motivated spouse, a secretary, or a billpayer service, what can you do to make the task more palatable?

The first step is to determine what is the best time for you to pay bills. Is it easier to pay them once or twice a month, or to pay each one as it arrives?

In the interest of financial planning, it is wiser to pay them once a month. This method gives you the opportunity to look at your overall financial picture, and to make financial decisions based on hard facts, rather than on feelings and fears. For example, if you know you can't pay all the credit card bills, you can choose the one with the highest interest rate and the highest balance to pay. However, if you know yourself well enough to recognize that you will procrastinate on a task that feels overwhelming—that is, facing a mountain of bills all at once—you may be better off paying each bill as it comes in.

A Place to Pay Up

Whatever method you decide to use, there are certain decisions you must make. If you pay bills at the office, establish a system for getting the bills from your mailbox to the office. Put them in a basket near the door, in a file on your desk, or directly into your briefcase. You can arrange to have the bills mailed directly to your office, if you wish.

If you pay your bills at home, choose where you will do it. The location must be a convenient one, if you are going to pay bills as they arrive. Otherwise it will be too much trouble to go there and you will not do it. If you pay bills once or twice a month, it is essential that you have a place to put the bills as they come in the mail. It is not essential that it be the same place you will eventually pay them. It is more important that the location be convenient, so you can get there easily when you are sorting the mail in the five minutes before you rush to pick up your daughter from soccer practice.

Be sure to have everything you need in your bill-paying location—stamps, envelopes, a pen that works, your checkbooks, and a place to put the receipts from the paid bills. Have a large wastebasket within reach for all those flyers with the "too good to be true" temptations! Finally, be sure to get the stamped bills to a place where you will see them, so that they actually get to the mailbox. Frequently amid my clients' piles of papers, I find checks they wrote, but never mailed! This is doubly frustrating, because it takes twice as long to pay next month's bill when you have to go through last month's records to see what you did or didn't pay. What's more, it is expensive to continually pay past due penalties.

Receipts: To Save or Not to Save

After you have paid the bills, then the question is, "What do I do with the receipts?" To answer that question, ask yourself another question: "What is the reason I would need this receipt?" If you recall your past habits, you may realize that you have indeed never used the information. You might then decide to throw them away, knowing that you can always refer to your cancelled checks and check register.

One possibility is to keep a record of payments to a particular company in case there are billing questions. Put the receipts in a file marked "MASTER CARD," or "SEARS," or a more generic file, "BILLS PAID."

Another function of such a file could be to provide a record of personal expenses. For example, you may keep records of expenditures on children in case a problem develops with child support. If so, create a file called "CHILD SUPPORT," "CHILDREN," or "FINANCIAL INFO—Children."

You may keep certain receipts for specific, but temporary, circumstances. For example, keep the utility bills, if you are planning to sell your home within the next year, because the information will interest a potential buyer. Frequently the primary reason for keeping the information is "For the IRS." (See Chapter 13 for detailed information.)

Another area of concern related to bills is the credit card receipt—those flimsy little pieces of paper stuffed in the pockets of your handbag, lying on top of your dresser and buried in your desk drawers. What should you do with them? One simple method is to get several business-size envelopes—one for each credit card and each bank account. If you have the space, hang the envelopes on a bulletin board with the flap tucked inside to create a pocket. Put the name of one credit card or bank account on each envelope. Then whenever you return from a shopping trip or making a bank deposit, put those receipts in the appropriate envelopes. Then, when the bank statement or credit card bill arrives, you can match them up in minutes!

Keep in mind that you only need to keep those receipts until you see that the purchase or deposits have been recorded accurately on your statement. Unless you want to keep them as receipts for a purchase, you can toss them!

Although you may not receive a paycheck to prove it, managing the financial records for a household is quite a job! Many people don't like to pay bills, but postponing the task doesn't make it easier or make it take less time. So take that first step and put every bill that comes in your mailbox in the "Pay" Action File. Then make an appointment with yourself, and do it.

13

The Tax Man Cometh

YOU CAN HATE paying taxes, think the tax system is unfair, dislike tax forms, and stage a mini-tax rebellion, but in the end the tax man cometh—with penalty! Undoubtedly April is one of the most traumatic months in every American household.

It's April 7. You haven't eaten in the dining room in two weeks. Shopping bags and shoe boxes of paid bills and receipts, piles of cancelled checks and unidentified cash register receipts cover the table. There are more receipts in the bottom of your briefcase, the back of the dresser drawer and on your kitchen counter. To add to the chaos, there is the 15-page guide from your accountant with instructions on what information is needed. Heads pound and stomachs churn as the countdown begins to April 15. What can you do to minimize the stress around this unavoidable deadline?

Two Kinds of Taxpayers

First, it is important to recognize that there are basically two kinds of taxpayers—those who feel comfortable only if they record deductions as they occur during the year, and those who prefer to ignore the entire issue until the fear of the penalty for late payment is greater than their willingness to procrastinate.

Somewhere in our education about managing our financial affairs, we heard the message that the *right* way to keep tax records is on a daily, or at least on some frequent, basis. We envision a professional-looking ledger with neat entries and accurate totals at the end of each month. Most of all we dream of walking into the tax accountant's office the first week of February with everything in order!

If you have never filed your taxes before April 15,

you are probably not the type of person who will conscientiously maintain daily records. Perhaps you should accept that as a reality, and plan accordingly!

There are *many* ways to maintain tax information. One man I know files all his receipts in two huge garbage bags—one labeled "Tax Deductible" and the other "Non-Tax Deductible." He then ignores the issue of taxes until the deadline hovers over him, and then digs in. Many people require a slightly more sophisticated system. Some people require a much more sophisticated system!

Determine your style of recordkeeping and weigh the alternatives for yourself. What are the risks of postponing the task? What is the worst possible thing that could happen? What would you do in that situation? Do you need an on-going system to feel secure? Is it reasonable to design a system that requires daily entries, or is it more realistic to accept the fact that you will not deal with taxes until April.

The April Approach

Remember that not all procrastination is necessarily negative. "Creative procrastination" can provide excellent motivation to do a job. It is possible, with certain preliminary precautions, to wait until April 15 is just around the corner, and still do the job effectively. In terms of time, it makes little difference whether you spend ten minutes a day, one hour per week, or three days once a year. If you recognize that waiting until the last minute is your normal approach, then accept it, and plan for it. Here's a game plan that should help you out.

Begin by collecting all the records you have—cancelled checks, credit card receipts and statements, bank statements, W-2 forms, 1099's, cash register receipts, calendars, your tax forms, and any articles or other information you may have collected about what you can deduct. Sort these papers into piles such as these:

general filing information and forms
proof of income
potential tax deductible categories
   contributions
   IRA contributions
   interest paid
   taxes paid
   medical and dental
   business expenses
   automobile
   entertaining
   travel
telephone
educational expense
professional dues & subscriptions

When all the papers have been separated into the appropriate pile, place each category into a separate container, such as a large envelope, plastic basket, or shoe box. Label each category clearly. Since you will probably need more than one sitting to complete your taxes, these labeled containers make it easier to clear your work area, if necessary, and to find your place when you are ready to continue.

Now take one category at a time. Eliminate duplicate receipts, such as your blue copy of the American Express charge or the copy sent with your monthly statement. Always keep the receipt with the most complete information, or staple the receipts together. If you need to correlate your charges with your calendar in order to prove a tax deductible expense, such as in the case of entertainment, put all receipts in chronological order to speed up the process.

Next, total the receipts and staple the adding machine tape to them. Write the category on the tape. You may want to make an itemized list of the deductions so your accountant can double check them, and so it will be easier to support your claim in the case of an audit.

Now you are ready to take your information to your accountant, or to begin entering the information on the forms yourself. Many accountants will provide a worksheet for compiling information.

Next year, if you decide again to postpone the agony until the last minute, be sure to allow enough time. The problem arises when you plan a business trip for early April and arrive home on April 13. Even if you manage to scrape together the necessary information, it is unlikely your accountant will be available—unless you have made previous arrangements. Your accountant is surely less effective after April 11. Rushed returns are usually incorrect!

The On-Going System

It is possible to avoid all the last-minute work if you so choose. What are the advantages of an on-going recordkeeping system?

For one thing, in the event of an audit, your chances of defending your deductions are greater if there is evidence that your expenses were noted "contemporaneously," as the IRS states it. Taxpayers are no longer permitted to recreate records months later to satisfy an audit, unless the records were destroyed in an extreme circumstance such as fire or flood. In addition, you are less likely to omit legitimate expenses if you record them as they occur.

You will be able to make better financial decisions, particularly if your income varies from month to month, as in the case of a self-employed individual. To live comfortably, it's not how much you earn, but how much you keep after taxes. The more records you have, the more claims you can prove, and the more money you will save. Taxpayers with incomplete records may pay Uncle Sam more than they legally owe. A real estate agent organized the paper in her home and discovered over $1500 of legitimate deductions she had failed to claim the previous year.

In the event your tax return is audited by the IRS, records are essential. Legitimate expenses may be disallowed for lack of documentation. If that is not enough to spur you into action, consider the high cost of interest and penalties on past due tax. Recordkeeping takes time and is not very exciting, but it does pay off, especially at tax time.

Finally, you can get your information to your tax accountant before the April rush. One client routinely filed a request for an extension on April 15 instead of filing his return. Last year, after filing his return early for the first time in his life, he received a refund on March 15! Instead of paying a penalty for non-payment of taxes, he received an interest payment on his savings account.

If you choose to keep your records as you go, make an appointment with yourself to get it done, whether at the end of each working day, or at the time you pay the monthly bills. If you record expenses on a calendar, choose one with enough space to write—or use a separate notebook. Do not allow perfectionism to defeat you. If you forget to record a luncheon expense at the time, decide what you can do next time. Beating yourself psychologically about your mistake does not improve the situation. A less than perfect recordkeeping system is better than no system at all!

Keep accurate records of income. IRS auditors frequently match deposit records to amounts declared on tax returns. If you cannot prove that a $2000 deposit is repayment of a loan to a friend by showing a copy of your original check or other transmittal, the IRS can treat the entire amount as taxable income. Note the source of the income on the deposit slip or in your check register.

Records of deductible items, such as medical bills, charitable donations, or casualty losses are best filed immediately. The system that demands the least amount of work at the end of the year has two clearly labeled envelopes for each category. One is for expenses paid by check or credit card. The information in this envelope will not be needed unless you are audited by the IRS and need additional supporting evidence. The second envelope is for cash receipts for the receipt is the only record. You will need to total this amount to add to your deductions. To simplify filing, arrange these envelopes in alphabetical order. For example, "DONATIONS—Check, Credit Card" and "DONATIONS—Cash" followed by "TRAVEL—Check, Credit Card" and "TRAVEL—Cash."

Experience demonstrates that, unless you are going to divide the information into exactly the same categories you will need on your tax return, it is not necessary to divide them at all. You will just have to duplicate your effort to divide them again when you are filing your return.

Crucial Steps

Regardless of your style, there are certain steps that are crucial. Make an appointment to see your tax consultant before April 15 to determine exactly what records you need to keep if it is not clear to you. This will eliminate unnecessary paper, and insure that you retain essential information.

Determine the particular place where you will keep any information relevant to filing your tax return, whether it is a dresser drawer, a file, a shoebox, a calendar or a computer.

Pay tax-deductible items by check or credit card whenever possible. At the end of the year, sorting cancelled checks and credit card receipts is much easier than sorting cash register receipts with blurred dates and miscellaneous unidentified scraps of paper. Some banks and brokerage firms even offer systems that break out taxable items paid by check. Computer software programs are also available for that purpose.

Ask yourself how much of your recordkeeping or tax preparation you really need or want to do yourself. Is there someone who can help—another family member, a secretary or a professional?

How Long Should You Keep Income Tax Records?

Ordinarily, the IRS is allowed three years from the date you filed your tax return, including extensions, to assess any additional tax. But a return can be audited for six years, if they suspect the taxpayer has neglected to report substantial income, or if they suspect fraud. Keep a copy of your return, W-2's, 1099's, and your cancelled checks showing payment permanently. Copies of gift tax returns should also be kept permanently. Put all information for one year in a separate envelope or box. After six years, discard all but essential documentation. (Many accountants say you are safe after three years.)

Before discarding any records, consider whether they are useful for another purpose, such as reducing capital gains on property sold. Be particularly careful with records relating to personal residence, other realty, all business property, and evidence of value of inherited property. There may be very good reasons to keep records longer than legally required, if you wish them for historical or reference purposes. However, it is crucial that you identify the reason for keeping these records. File them by asking the question, "What word would I think of if I wanted this information?" (See Chapter 10.)

14

Family Records

A VIRGINIA FATHER had to revaccinate his 5-year old to enter school because he couldn't find the immunization card and the doctor who did it was no longer in practice. A business executive missed an important financial opportunity because she needed to fly to Italy and couldn't find her passport. A financially struggling widow lost over $2000 in medical insurance reimbursements because she didn't file the claims within the two-year time limit.

What if you, your spouse, or both of you suddenly died or became incapacitated? Who knows where to find your will or what insurance benefits you have? What about the key to your safe deposit box? Could anyone find the cash stashed away in a money market fund?

If any of these questions makes you feel uneasy, it is essential that you organize your records. In so doing, you will be able to identify areas that need attention, such as out-of-date wills, inadequate homeowner's insurance, missing legal documents, or a beneficiary change you need to make on your insurance policy.

Bank Records

Your files should include the name and address of each bank, credit union, or savings and loan association, type of account, account number, certificate number, signers on the account and location of passbooks, statement or certificate.

Many banks block joint accounts when they receive notification of death of one of the joint owners. If this is the case, each spouse may wish to set up a separate emergency account in his or her own name. It is a good idea to ask your bank to write you a letter stating its policy, so you know beforehand.

Education, Employment and Military Records

A separate file should be kept for each member of the family. For example, "Education Records—Susan," "Education Records—Paul," and "Military Records—Bob." The information in these files simplify the task of writing or rewriting a resume, applying for admission to an education institution, submitting an application for an award, or applying for a new job. Besides, who knows—someone may want to write your biography one day.

Family History Records

The purpose of this category is to assemble in one place important family information which might be necessary to obtain a passport, apply for social security and veterans benefits, or to file a loan application. For each family member include birthdate (copy of birth certificate if available; original should be in safe deposit box), social security number, copy of marriage or divorce certificate. Any family genealogy records can also be kept here.

Include in the Family History Records file the name and phone number for your accountant, financial planner, employee-benefits advisor, insurance agents (life, health, car, personal property, homeowners), stockbroker, or other financial advisor.

Household Inventory

One of the most neglected family records is the household inventory. A client purchased a $15,000 painting, but neglected to add it to his insurance policy. When the repair person accidently damaged it, the owner had to pay for repairs himself. If there is a fire or burglary in your home, this record will help you remember what has to be replaced and determine the value of each item. An inventory is also an excellent way to make certain that your insurance protection is sufficient.

When you make an inventory, start at one point in the room and go all the way around, listing everything. The more complete the information, the more valuable it will be. Include information such as initial cost, model numbers, brand names, and descriptions. Take photographs of the room and special items so that identifying or replacing them will be easier. Be sure to include the basement, garage and attic. If you estimate the replacement cost for each item, add up the total, and you will know what your insurance should cover. Videotapes make excellent inventories. At the same time you are taking inventory, it is a good idea to mark your property with some identification. Your local police department may have a special identification program. You can also purchase engravers to mark items with your social security number.

Update your inventory every six months or so by adding new purchases and adjusting replacement costs. Some insurance policies do that automatically. Be sure you know the limits in your homeowner's policy with regard to valuables such as jewelry, furs, and art.

If you find the task of preparing a household inventory overwhelming, check your yellow pages and find a professional to do it, or get other members of the family to help you. Be sure to keep the records in a fireproof safe at home, a bank safe deposit box, or at some off-site location.

Insurance Records

The information about your policies are important for two reasons. In the event of your death, it ensures that your family and executor of your estate will know what insurance benefits are available, which companies and insurance agents to contact and how to file claims. In addition, should you become incapacitated due to accident or illness, your family will be able to pay policy premiums to keep your coverage in force. Periodically, it is essential to evaluate the adequacy of your coverage.

Insurance

The life insurance policies themselves should be in your safe deposit box, but your active files at home should identify the name of the company for each policy, the policy number, face amount, beneficiaries, whether there has been a loan taken on the policy, premium due date, and the name of the agent. Determine whether your coverage is adequate to protect your dependents and assets.

Automobile Insurance

Since so much time is spent in automobiles, it is important to know your automobile liability insurance is sufficient. Is your automobile overinsured for collision? Do you wish to increase the deductible in order to reduce the premium? Will your coverage protect you if you are driving a rental car, or if someone else is driving your car? Keep the policy in your active file for easy accessibility.

Medical Insurance Records

Do you have major medical insurance with high limits? Do you have adequate disability insurance? One of the greatest insurance concerns for many people is getting reimbursed for medical expenses.

The simplest, most effective way to keep track of the status of insurance claims is to create three file folders. The first is labeled "Medical Insurance—To be Submitted." This contains the blank claim forms, the instructions on how to submit a claim, and any receipts from the doctor, laboratory, clinic, or pharmacy. The second file folder is labeled, "Medical Insurance—Submitted, But not Paid." This contains a photocopy of the patient copy of any claims you submitted for reimbursement, but for which you have not yet received payment. Finally, the third folder is labeled, "Medical Claims—Paid." This information should be kept for three years to support any information in the IRS return.

Every insurance claim is in one of these three stages. Therefore, it is very simple to check on the status of any claim at any time, as it moves through the system.

Medical Records

In addition to insurance records, it is important to keep individual medical records. The simplest method is to establish a file labeled "Medical—Mary" and "Medical—John." Include receipts from doctors and dentists which identify diseases and treatments (these can be culled from the "Health Insurance—Paid" file). Information about blood type, eyeglass prescriptions, and allergies can also be useful.

Finally, many people like to keep articles about medical *developments* or pamphlets they pick up at the doctor's office or the pharmacy. Do not include this information in your medical records file. Make a separate file called "Medical Information—General." If it becomes too bulky to handle, separate it into various areas of concern, e.g., "Medical Information—Cancer" or "Medical Information—Coronary Care."

Investment Records

While the monetary rewards resulting from investments can create a great sense of security, the paper created by those investments often creates a great sense of insecurity for many people! One of my clients had a four-drawer filing cabinet full of annual reports from the past thirteen years. She had never read one of them, but she was convinced she should keep them, just in case! Many of the papers sent to you by an investment company are intended to inform you of their recommendations for stock purchases, to meet regulatory requirements, and to keep you abreast of the status of the companies in which you have invested. Keep a separate file for essential information, including your monthly statements and the confirmations of your various buy and sell transactions, as opposed to the generic information which is sent to all investors.

Stocks and bonds: Where are the certificates kept? List name and address of brokers, list of holdings, including owner's name, date bought and purchase price for each stock and bond.

Keogh's/IRA's: For each family member, include name of institution and location of papers.

Other investments:

Collectibles: What kind? Kept where? Who should appraise for sale?

Tax Shelters: Type; documents kept where? Particulars?

Businesses: Type; where? Documents kept where? Whom to contact?

In most families, one person handles most financial matters. If you've been the family controller, you know the intricacies of the situation. Continuity in planning and implementing financial strategies is important, and while you can't expect someone else to follow your exact track, you want your successor to understand what you have been doing. This means that in addition to listing where the assets are, you should provide information on managing any complicated situations to help a beginner take charge of your affairs.

Liabilities Records

There are two primary reasons for keeping a complete liabilities record. First, should you become ill and require hospitalization, your family should know not only to whom you owe money, but also when payments are due to avoid unnecessary complications. Second, should you die, a comprehensive record of your liabilities serves as a basis to dismiss any false claims made against your estate.

Include installment debts on home(s), automobile, home improvements, personal loans, furniture, appliances, business loans. Information needed is current balance, monthly payment, due date, and whether there is debt insurance.

Credit Cards and Charge Accounts

List account numbers and names of issuers so that survivors can notify issuers if the cards have been lost or stolen, or if the accounts are to be closed or listed in a different name.

Real Estate Records

Property separately owned and jointly owned by married persons should be clearly indicated. If the joint owner is other than a spouse, give the name, address, and interest of each joint owner.

Include the name and address of the mortgagee, how titled, date of acquisition and cost, mortgage terms including the original amount, the monthly payment and the payment due date, and date of final payment.

Retirement Income Records

In planning ahead for retirement it is extremely important for you and your spouse to have a complete up-to-date record of your pension plan or plans, any annuities you will receive, rents or royalties, and your estimated social security benefits. You can obtain a leaflet "Estimating Your Social Security Check" from your nearest social security office, and you can obtain a statement of your social security earnings by sending a "Request for Statement of Earnings" form to the Social Security Administration. These forms are available from your local office.

Warranties and Instructions

One of the major joys or major frustrations of the American kitchen in the 20th century is the kitchen gadget. It is a joy when you can find it when you need it, but a major frustration when you can't remember how to operate it—and you can't find the instruction book!

Every time you purchase a new appliance, toy, tool, or other household item, you are blessed with several new pieces of paper: a consumer registration card, a promotional brochure for other products manufactured by the same company, an instruction booklet, and frequently, a consumer questionnaire. To further complicate matters, often a company will issue the same warranty for several products. Just because you can find a warranty doesn't mean you will know what it protects!

To minimize this problem, there are several steps you can take.

(1) Decide where you will keep all warranty and instructional information. (I do not recommend separating them, because often one piece of paper will have the warranty and the instruction.) You may decide to keep those related to kitchen appliances in the kitchen, so they will be readily available, or if your kitchen storage space is limited, you may choose to put them in the household filing system under "Warranties and Instructions." Frequently it is helpful to put instruc-

tion booklets with a stereo, telephone, or tape recorder so you can refer to it easily. Instructions relating to clothing could be kept in a plastic bag in the laundry room.

(2) Whenever you make a purchase, staple the receipt to the warranty information so you can easily prove date of purchase or put the date on the front of the warranty for your own info.

(3) Decide now whether you will or will not fill out consumer information cards and warranty registration cards. Frequently we take longer shuffling the card than it would take to fill out the card! Usually, it is not required in order to make the warranty valid, but it is helpful to manufacturers and is essential if you need to be reached for product recall.

Safe Deposit Box

Papers that are difficult or impossible to replace should be kept in a safe deposit box. It should be large enough to hold everything that should be in it—and small enough to keep out things that do not need to be there. The box should not be used as a catchall for souvenirs.

Certain documents you should keep in your safe deposit box:

—Adoption papers
—Automobile titles
—Birth certificates
—Citizenship papers
—Copies of wills (Original, in most cases, should be kept with County Registrar of Wills)
—Death certificates
—Divorce decrees
—Government or court recorded documents

—Household inventory and negatives from pictures
(include appraisals and receipts)
—Important contracts
—Leases
—Life insurance policies
—List of insurance policy names and numbers
—Marriage certificate
—Military records
—Passports
—Patents and copyrights
—Property deed and other mortgage papers
—Retirement plans
—Stock and bond certificates and notes

Keep a list of everything you have in your safe deposit box (in your active files at home). Be sure to
update the list as you add or remove items.

If you store documents from investment properties
or securities, the rental can be claimed as a deduction
on your income tax return.

Finally, make sure family members know where the
box is located and the key is kept.

Survivors' Benefits Records

Tragically, many survivor's benefits are left un-
claimed because the survivors are unaware of their
availability. These benefits are not paid automatically.
Applications must be made on prescribed forms and
specific documents furnished.

Apply at the local Social Security Administration office for benefits to which you may be entitled. The
Veterans Administration offers several types of benefits to the survivors of deceased veterans or of active
duty service personnel. These benefits do not conflict
with claims made under Social Security, but again, they

are not paid automatically. In most cases, claims must be made within two years following death.

There are several other possible sources of survivor's benefits including Worker's Compensation, Employer's Insurance Policy, Life Insurance Policy, Health/Accident Policy, Auto/Casualty Insurance, Trade Union, and Fraternal Organizations. Be sure you family is aware of these benefits, and include phone numbers where they can get information.

Tax Records

Be sure that family members know where to locate information for filing income tax returns (See Chapter 14).

Trusts

List any trusts you have created or any trusts created by others under which you possess any power, beneficial interest, or trusteeship. Include the name of the trust, location, trustee and beneficiary.

Your Will

For couples, the importance of both parties having up-to-date wills cannot be overemphasized. The individual who makes no will forfeits any assurance that his or her property will be distributed according to his or her wishes, and will probably cause unnecessary difficulties and possible financial losses for the survivors. When a person dies without a will, the distribution of the estate is governed by state laws which may not fit the best interest of your family.

Review your will periodically. If you have married, divorced, remarried, or if heirs have been born or died, if the size or nature of your estate has changed, or if you have moved to a different state, your will needs to be updated.

In Case of Ill or Aging Family Members

Admittedly, this is one of the most difficult areas of paper management, but it is also one of the most important. In addition to making sure your own records are in order, be sure you have or know where to get the information for any family members for whom you are responsible. You will need a Power of Attorney if that person dies, or becomes unable to make his/her own decisions.

By planning ahead of time, some of the stress involved when a family member dies can be eliminated.

For a burial permit, you will need to know the vital statistics of the deceased:

Name, home address and telephone number
How long in state
Name of business, address and telephone
Occupation and title
Social security number
Armed Service serial number
Date and place of birth
Citizenship
Father's name and birthplace
Mother's maiden name and birthplace

You will need certain documents regarding the deceased:

Death certificate (certificates for burial permit, insurance, etc.)
Will
Birth Certificate or other legal proof of age

Social Security Card
Marriage and Divorce Certificates, if any
Citizenship papers, if naturalized
Military discharge papers
Insurance policies
Bank books
Deeds to property, automobile title(s)
Income tax returns
Disability claims

You will need to notify certain persons:

Doctor or Health Maintenance Organization
Funeral director or memorial society
Institution to which remains may be donated if living will exists
Memorial park
Relatives, friends, employers of deceased
Insurance agents
Attorney, accountant or executor of estate
Religious, fraternal, civic, veteran's groups
Newspapers regarding death notices

Changes in records need to be made for automobile title, stocks and bonds, and bank accounts.

A friend of mine said she felt so badly when her mother died because she did not know whether she wanted her wedding ring left on when she was buried. Be sure to include any special instructions to the family about your memorial service, funeral, or burial preferences. It will be a big comfort to your family.

15

Family Memorabilia and Photographs

IT'S SEPTEMBER. THE summer vacations, family gatherings, and neighborhood barbecues were great fun. But all that remain are the warm memories, thirty-seven envelopes of photographs, and thirteen video-tapes that pop up like mushrooms all over the house, but are nowhere to be found when you want to show them to someone! Add to that the boxes of old family photographs and unidentified snapshots your mother passed on to you for safekeeping, the trunk of family memorabilia you married along with your husband, the piles of artistic creativity your children produce, and the photos and memorabilia you have collected from family travels over the years (including when you were in high school and college), and there seems to be no relief in sight.

It Only Seems Hopeless

When you consider the amount of love, time, and money that have gone into these artifacts thus far, you feel obligated to do something. The question is,

"What?" It is obvious that the simple baby books and photo albums like those our mothers used are no longer adequate for most families. Your intentions are good, but the mechanics of the task seem overwhelming—and where do you find the time, even if you have the motivation? How do you begin? And what if you don't have the motivation? Can you risk ignoring the issue? And what about the space it takes in your house which you could be using for something else?

The most important step in changing all this is for you to recognize that the situation, if left unchecked, is only going to get worse. As life goes on, the memorabilia continues to accumulate. If the old stuff is out of control, just think what another year's worth will be like!

In order to begin making progress on this seemingly impossible task, start now—not with those piles of yesterday's memories, but with those you collect today. You can work on the backlog after you have devised a system that works for you.

Make It Easy On Yourself

The next step is to recognize that you will probably not have the time to do the task as perfectly as you would like to. Don't let that perfectionism stop you. What is important is to determine what you are willing and able to do, and to do it. Accept the fact that you may not want, or be able to do it the way your mother or father did. That does not mean you are a failure. It only means that you have different priorities at this time in your life.

Design a system to fit *your* particular needs. Start by identifying an accessible place where you will put all the memorabilia as you receive it or find it. If you have a small amount, two boxes labeled "Photographs" and "Memorabilia" (napkins, brochures, invitations, matchbooks, dried flowers, etc.) may be all that you will need. If you have difficulty putting things away in their proper place, leave the lids off the boxes so they will be easier for you to use. At the end of the year, put the lids on the boxes. Be sure that the outside of the boxes are clearly labeled, "Photos—1987," and put them away. If you are short on storage space, put your boxes in an out-of-the-way location, such as the attic or basement. Then note on the file index (See Chapter 10) where they are.

Take whatever steps you can to make the organization process *easier*. If you don't have time to go through and label each picture, make a note on the outside of the photo envelope as to the major categories, "Summer—1965," or "Jerry's Birthday Party—1987." You might also have your photos developed at a lab that dates the back of your photos (You can even purchase a camera attachment which dates the photo when you take it!). Put a date on memorabilia such as travel brochures, napkins, etc. as you receive it. You will be able to recreate the occasion more easily if you decide to organize the materials in some more sophisticated style.

If you are a "memoraholic," you may need to divide your treasures into smaller categories to make them more manageable. There are several ways you can do that. For example, if you have more than one child, you may wish to have a photo album or memorabilia box for each child. Or, you may want to create categories by type such as "Children's Art," "Playbills," "Trips." These can be further broken down by destination and date, such as "Europe—1980."

Feelings, Feelings

One of the major problems with photographs and other memorabilia is all the emotion involved. Even if we have no interest in them ourselves, we feel that we should have, because they represent our family history. How do you know what is your heritage while you are living it? We feel burdened because they were so important to our parents, or because they might be important to our yet unborn grandchildren. In the meantime, what do we do with them? They fill our attics and basements with boxes and our minds with guilt.

If you are facing that dilemma, there are several steps you can take to ease the problem. First, recognize that there is not a right or wrong approach to this problem. In order to decide what you want to do, begin gathering information about the alternatives you may have. Determine who else might be involved in the decision-making process.

Keep in mind that it is not possible to foresee exactly how your descendants will feel about this information. You can only make your decisions based on your current information and resources.

Kids Can Get Involved, Too

If you have children who are old enough to be involved in the decision-making, ask them how they feel about the issue. You can give family memorabilia to your children, but be sure to do so with "no strings attached." Let them decide what to do with it based on their own needs and perspectives. If you feel strongly about what should happen, and will be hurt if they do not do it, keep it yourself, or find someone who agrees with your wishes.

Perhaps it is not important to them, nor to you. Then your best solution may be to ask a professional buyer of memorabilia to determine whether there is anything of value to other people. You may feel better if you get more than one opinion, but if that involves too much trouble, accept that fact and go on with the things in your life which are more important to you.

If you or your children feel it is important to go through everything yourselves in order to determine what you should keep, then you will need to develop a system for doing that. When time is a major factor, you may find it necessary or desirable to hire a professional organizing consultant to help you with the task. If your children think it should be done, get a commitment from them as to how and when they will help.

Doing It Alone

If you are going to do it alone, make a plan for yourself as to how you can best accomplish the task. Will you have to do it in bits and pieces, or is it possible to spend several days working on the project? In either event, set goals for yourself. When you are having guests for dinner after work, you can fix dinner in an hour when you need to, but when you have all day Saturday, you can spend hours preparing dinner. This project works the same way. The more time you allow, the more it will take.

If you have a home with plenty of storage space, your decisions about what to keep may be different than someone who lives in a small apartment. Off-site storage is a possibility if you have no space in your home, but you have some things you wish to keep. Be sure to compare prices when choosing one. Decide whether it is important that the belongings be stored close to your neighborhood, or whether you can use a storage facility some distance from your home, which may save you money.

If you're having trouble parting with some items, but don't have enough space, consider ways of using memorabilia in you home or office. Thanks to the help of a creative friend, I now enjoy decorating with many memorabilia treasures that used to be buried in drawers, taking up room and never seen or enjoyed.

One of the questions I always ask clients when they are deciding whether or not to keep a particular object is, *"How does it make you feel?"* If the answer is guilty, sad, angry, or any other negative emotion, ask yourself why you are choosing to surround yourself with these feelings. Then decide on positive action you can take.

Memorabilia Scrapbooks

It is my experience that memorabilia scrapbooks for special mementos other than photographs, require a great deal of patience and creativity, since many of them come in odd shapes and sizes. If you enjoy such projects, you can have a ball, but if you don't, it is probably unrealistic to expect much success at doing it. I recommend just leaving the items in your "Memorabilia Box."

The Knack of Good Photo-Albuming

If you have taken all, or even some, of the steps described thus far, don't be surprised if one day you discover you really are ready to get those photographs into albums. It's a terrific project when you are housebound for one reason or another. First of all, do take whatever steps you can to get into the right frame of mind. Look on the process as a wonderful adventure into memory land. Get into comfortable clothes, put on your favorite music, fix a pot of coffee (but don't put it where you risk ruining any photographs if it spills!), and you're on your way. Then take the following steps:

1. Choose a place to work with a clean, flat surface and plenty of light where you can leave the project until it is completed—or at least long enough to make some major progress. (Resist the urge to rush out and buy photo albums at this point! Time will give you a better idea of the kind and quantity you need.)

2. Sort through your photos and eliminate all those unsuccessful shots. Don't be discouraged—even professional photographers use only a small percentage of the photos they take. The first candidates for

the wastebasket are double exposures and those fascinating shots of the inside of your lens cap! Very close behind are those pictures you wish had been double exposures—like the one that shows only the lower half of your body, and those shots you wonder why you took (the one of the Christmas tree after you took down the decorations!).

3. Give away those photos that have little meaning to you, but could be special to someone else. They are fun to drop in the mail, and you will undoubtedly bring a quick smile to Aunt Amanda's face!

4. Before you separate the pictures from their negatives, write a description on the outside of the packet, such as "Graduation—John, 1987," or simply use dates. You may decide that once you have the picture and as many copies as you want, you can throw the negatives away. If you want an "insurance policy" against unexpected disasters, such as theft, fire, divorce, or other loss, keep the negatives in a separate place. Your mother's house or a safe deposit box are two possibilities.

5. Determine whether you are going to put the information about the photo on the back of the photo itself, or on a separate piece of paper so that it could be read after the photos are in albums. (Some energetic people do both!) The more information you know, the more joy the photo will bring in the years to come—who, what, where, when, and why. Experience has proven that, while a picture may be worth a million words, an unidentified picture is worth little to future generations.

6. Sort photos into the categories you plan to use in the albums. Most people do it chronologically, but some people do it by subject matter—for example, "Family Reunions." CAUTION: Label the piles as you

work. Then, if you are interrupted, it will not take long to proceed with the sorting. One easy way to do this is to purchase inexpensive small baskets which can be labeled temporarily with "Post-It Notes" or "Post-It Tape."

7. Now is the time to decide what kind of albums you wish to use. A loose-leaf photograph album has a distinct advantage if you are trying to arrange photos chronologically, because it will be easy to add a page if you find more photos after you finish the project.

If you want to limit the number of photo albums you will need, you may prefer the kind in which the photos are in individual sleeves, overlapping one another. The disadvantage of this type is that it will not accommodate over-sized photos.

8. Let your creativity loose! Enjoy experimenting with different arrangements. Feel free to trim photos to their best advantage. If you have several photos from one event, group them together on one or more pages, and write a short scenario about the occasion, rather than labeling each photo individually.

Slides, Films, and Tapes

Slides to organize? Label in pen directly on the cardboard frame. Label so that you can look at the slide with the naked eye and read the label at the same time. This will be a big advantage should you ever want to put together a slide show.

Movies or videotapes should be organized, too. The key is to label them clearly. Keep peel-off labels and a felt-tipped pen in the same drawer or shelf as you keep your photographic equipment. Label as you go—even if you don't have time to do it perfectly.

Be Creative

As you browse through your photos, consider ways of using your favorites in some unusual way. Check with your local photographic supply or film processing shop for ideas. Some possibilities are:

1. Make your own picture postcards. "Photo Talk" stickers are available from a photographic supply store. You can use these stickers to add amusing comments above people's heads.

2. Make a photo T-shirt. Take a color slide or color print that is the size you want to a copy shop that has a heat transfer machine. Apply the transfer to a T-shirt just as you would an iron-on patch.

3. Make a jigsaw puzzle. Companies advertise this service in the classified section of a magazine, or check your local photo finishing store. A great gift idea!

4. Make a poster. Turn your pictures into artwork to hang in your family room or college dorm room. Consider panoramic views of places that are special to you. The same companies that make jigsaw puzzles can do this for you.

5. Make a calendar. Custom photo-finishing labs are equipped to print a photo above a twelve-month calendar. A great holiday gift idea for friends or business associates.

6. Make a videotape from a slide show. Some photography stores will do this, or your video store may be able to refer you to an individual who specializes in custom-made videotapes from slides.

The next time a grandparent or other elderly family member is celebrating a birthday or other special occasion, and you cannot think of a suitable present, ask him or her if they have any old photographs. Chances are they will, and nothing would please them more than to have your help in putting them in albums. My grandmother talked for years about all the photographs she had never labeled. She was concerned that she couldn't remember everything about the pictures, and that her handwriting was not good enough for future generations. So I invited her to tell me about the photos, while I made notes. Eventually I found at least one picture of every member in both grandparent's families. Whenever anyone comes to visit, it takes her only a few minutes to find the photo album. And the reminiscing begins. Who received the greatest gift is still not clear.

Keep Those Cards and Letters Coming

What do you do about all those beautiful greeting cards you have received for birthdays, anniversaries, and other special events? What about all the letters from relatives and friends? If you keep them, you feel guilty because they take up so much room, and if you toss them, you feel guilty because you care about the people who sent them, they cost so much money, or you just think they are too pretty to throw away!

There is nothing wrong with keeping every card and letter you ever receive if you have plenty of space to store them and you enjoy looking at them, or just entertaining the possibility that you might someday! If, however, you feel a knot in your stomach every time you see them, or you don't have a place to put the stationery you need for answering today's mail, then you would be wise to reconsider your actions.

One viable solution for letters is to select the ones that contain information which would be of particular interest in the future. I enjoy saving the letters from my mother which describe special family events, for example.

The method you use for keeping cards and letters

will be determined by the way you plan to use them. If you are keeping them strictly for casual reading in the years to come, a box labeled "Letters to Save" will do nicely. If, however, you want to be able to refer to them, for any reason, you may want to file them alphabetically in an accordian-type file with alphabet dividers.

I put all the cards I receive for a particular occasion on the mantle in the family room. After two or three weeks, I keep only those which are particularly special—and in some cases I throw them all away because I know there are others, and I am optimistic enough to believe there will be more! A friend of mine keeps all of hers, and then every few years makes a collage of them to hang as a decoration. Some community groups collect them to use in self-help projects for handicapped persons and senior citizens. Sometimes schools are happy to have them for art projects.

Whatever you decide to do with them, remember that the sender intended that card or letter to bring joy, not stress—so enjoy!

16

Your "To Read" Pile

ONE OF THE major challenges of paper management is the "To Read" pile. Books, magazines, newspapers, journals relating to professional interests, as well as personal interests, newsletters from the organizations we belong to, self-help newsletters to which we subscribe, and promotional materials which describe insurance policies that interest us, self-improvement materials we can purchase, awards we may have won, or candidates for political office whom we support, fill our lives. Even the guides which come for our cable television, and the instructions for our latest gadget require reading. I purchased a window fan for my bedroom, only to discover I couldn't turn it on until I read the instructions about how to program the timer!

In many cases, the real issue of "To Read" is *not* to read, but to *remember*. We are afraid that we might miss something that could be very important to our lives, or at least be a lot of fun! We want to be "well-read" in order to make a good impression on our friends and business colleagues.

There is a very positive aspect to an overflowing

Alternate Uses for Unread Books.

"To Read" pile. We have many interests, which is what makes us interesting, productive, and creative people. Remember that *a creative mind always has more ideas than the body can carry out.* Many of those ideas come from what we read, but what we must also remember is that there is no shortage of resources for ideas. There will always be more magazines and more newspapers. Spend your time reading, not feeling guilty over what you haven't read.

Be Selective

The first step in solving the problem is to accept the fact that it is unlikely that you will ever be able to read all the things you think you ought to read, let alone all the things you would like to read—even if you do take the best speed reading course the country has to offer! The law of rising expectations will undoubtedly prevail. If you increase the speed at which you can read, the amount of information you want to read will also increase. So, although completing a speedreading course may be a desirable goal, it will not solve the problem of the ever-growing "To Read" pile.

The issue is not reading faster, but reading smarter. One of the first rules is to be more selective. Check the table of contents for articles that relate to your specific interest, instead of just browsing through a magazine or journal. Read lead paragraphs, lead sentences, and closing paragraphs to get the main idea. Beware of the lures of modern day marketing! Do you catch yourself reading a publication or major advertising promotion, just because the promoter made it look so appealing, while at the same time ignoring a publication you must read in order to be current in the literature of your field?

Play a game with yourself to see how much potential reading material can go directly into the wastebasket before it hits your "To Read" pile. If the temptation to read materials that are not applicable to your situation is too overwhelming, take yourself off mailing and circulation lists. Have your secretary, or your spouse, if he or she is agreeable, screen your mail and throw away, file, or reroute those items you do not need to read. Be particularly leery of those publications you receive as business perks. Ask yourself, "If I were paying for this publication out of my own pocket, would I still order it?" If not, cancel it, or give it to someone who would benefit more from the subscription.

Make an inventory of the magazines and periodicals you receive each month. Estimate the amount of time it would take to read them the way you expect yourself to do it. Are your expectations realistic? If not, what can you do about it? Identify which publications contribute the most value. Consider alternating subscriptions every year or two.

Improve Your Technique

When you have eliminated absolutely everything your personality will allow, then begin to improve your reading techniques. One of the major stumbling blocks in reducing the "To Read" pile is perfectionism. For example, you receive an alumni newsletter in the mail. You are honestly interested in the news of your former classmates, but there simply isn't time to read it now. So you put it on the credenza behind your desk or in the basket beside your lounge chair in the family room. And guess what? Six months later it is still there, along with the other four issues! Or, you receive a newsletter from your professional association. You feel obligated to keep up on the latest happenings, and there are some activities in which you would like to participate, but there's no time to read it now. So in the basket it goes. By the time you get around to it a month later, the seminar which really suited your needs is already filled, or the date has passed. Or, you become tired of seeing the piles and toss them all out. In either event, they end up in the wastebasket, serving no purpose except to create clutter and guarantee guilt!

What can you do to solve this perennial problem? *If your "To Read" pile is too high, you have two options: (1) Read it or (2) Throw it away.* If you do not choose the latter, then you face a time management problem. There is only one way to read, and that is to put aside the time to do it. This means setting aside the time on your calendar. There are no magic words to make the pile disappear. Make an appointment with yourself to read, just as you would make an appointment with someone else to go to the movies.

Consider your own biological rhythms. Is it easier to get up an hour earlier, or stay up an hour later? Can you take a sack lunch to work two days a week and read through your lunch hour? Does your work situation allow you to set aside a "quiet time" each day, or two to three times a week, when your secretary will screen out all but the most important calls?

Incorporate

Look for creative ways to incorporate reading into your daily life. Can you use public transportation, or a car pool to get to work, and use that time for reading? Do you travel frequently? If so, designate a place to put reading materials you can take with you on your next trip. Then use those inevitable delays as a gift of reading time, instead of a total disaster. Do you drive a car pool for your children and end up waiting for them, spend time waiting in doctor's offices, or go to meetings which frequently begin late? Always carry with you reading material so you can make the time productive if you want to. (I am not suggesting that every uncommitted moment should be spent reading—or anything else. Sometimes the best way to use a few unexpected moments is to do some deep breathing or fantasize about a day at the beach!) However, if you carry reading material with you, you can make a conscious choice instead of finding yourself in an unconscious trap. Keep in mind that it can be "fun reading!" One client of mine loves to read spy novels. He always carries one with him on airplanes—the only time he enjoys that relaxation luxury.

Categorize Your Reading

Separate your reading into types of reading. For example, many people enjoy reading mail order catalogs when they want to relax. If so, put a basket beside your bed where you can collect them. When the basket gets full, that is your signal that it is time to toss some out—or start over completely. If, however, you are a serious catalog shopper, you will need to take steps to insure that your catalog browsing is productive. Write on the front cover of the catalog the name and page number of the item in which you are interested. Or, tear out that page, but be sure to jot down the phone number you will need for ordering, or tear out the mail order form.

Another category might be the materials you would like to read, but which are not high priority, and which will be outdated at a specific time. Jot down on the cover the deadline date for reading. Then go through the pile periodically and throw out the ones that are too old. This category of reading is a good one to carry with you when you travel because you can take advantage of the added incentive of lightening your luggage! Give yourself a "statute of limitations" of this category. If you haven't read it in six weeks, throw it out!

Separate out the high priority reading, so that when you have set aside reading time you will not be tempted by the lower priority category.

Use Your Reference Files

Many people are hesitant to file away an article that they have not read because they are afraid it "may not be worth it." My experience has made it clear that we are more apt to read those articles that relate to the issues which are of particular importance at the moment. For example, if you find an article on planning a birthday party for a five-year-old, and your son just turned four, your motivation to read the article will not be very great, but if his birthday is two weeks away, you will be very interested in the information. When you find an article that interests you, and you don't have time to read it, tear out the article and file it according to the topic it relates to. Then when you are dealing with the issue it will be much easier to determine whether the article is of any importance. If the article remains in the pile of magazines behind your credenza, it is highly unlikely that you will remember you have it, let alone have the time to go through the pile of magazines to find it!

One of the most effective ways to utilize the information you accumulate is to create your own reference library. *Ask yourself, "If I wanted this information again, what word would I think of?"* The answer to that question is the title of your reference file.

If this situation arises frequently, you may find it necessary to create a reference file separate from the rest of your files. (See Chapter 10). However if it happens infrequently, you can incorporate the article into your existing file system. For example, an article on how to choose a caterer could go in your "Entertaining" file. An article on antique restorers could go in "Decorating" or "House Information."

Always read with a pen in your hand. If you are reading a magazine, and discover an article you would like to save, but you can't tear it out because your spouse hasn't read it, or there is another article of interest on the other side, just note the page number of the article (and the subject, if you wish) on the front cover. Then, months from now, when you are faced with stacks of old magazines, you will be able to identify very quickly which contain articles you want to keep. (You may also discover some articles which interest you less now than they did when you marked them!)

Set Limits

One of the most common questions from clients is "How long should I keep books, newspapers, and magazines?" There is no right or wrong answer to this question. The answer depends entirely upon your feelings about these publications. For example, some people enjoy being around books, whether or not they have read them, or ever intend to read them. They appreciate books the way other people appreciate art or scenic views. If you feel that way about books, and you have plenty of bookshelf space, then by all means keep them. If however, like me, unread books create stress, then eliminate those you have read once and do not intend to read again, those given to you by well-meaning friends and relatives (even if they did cost a fortune!), eliminate those you picked up off the "Under $2.00" shelf in the local bookstore, and make an appointment with yourself to read the remaining ones!

What about magazines and newspapers? Again, there is no right or wrong answer. Look at each publication individually, and make a decision about how long you will keep it. For example, if you have young children, you may feel compelled to keep your *National Geographics* as reference material for future school projects. If you are a gourmet cook or entertain frequently, you may decide to keep *Gourmet* permanently. News magazines, however, are of little value when they are more than a week or two old, unless you happen to be a historian or a journalist.

I use the Sunday paper as my signal that it is time to discard the previous week's papers. If there are articles I really want to read but did not get around to it, they are torn from the paper and filed in the reference file as discussed earlier in this chapter. You may wish to photocopy newspaper articles. They can be reduced in size and therefore take up less file space. In addition, the photocopy will last longer than a newspaper copy.

Identify those items that are of extremely limited value when they become outdated. Last week's *TV Guide*, old phone books, catalogs from stores you've never ordered from, and last month's *Newsweek* are primary candidates for the trash!

If you really enjoy holding on to publications, what is the best way to do it? The first step is the same one we use in organizing so many things: *"Put like objects together."* For example, all travel books together, all kitchen magazines together, all catalogs together. If you like, put colored dots on book bindings to make it easy to keep them in the appropriate category. Put magazines in cardboard or plastic magazine holders—labeled with name and year of publication.

When you see the amount of one category you have accumulated, you can determine whether you really want to take up that much of your living space with that item. You may wish to create a card file, alphabetized by subject, so you can note a particular book, magazine, or article that interested you. Then if it becomes important, you can easily retrieve it at your local library. If you do not want a separate system, put the information in an existing file on that subject or inside another book you already have on the subject.

After you have categorized all your reading material and eliminated any that you decide is excess, the final step is to designate a place to keep it. To determine that, ask yourself where you would be most likely to read or otherwise utilize the information. If it is reference material, in what room would you be most likely to look for it? Travel and foreign language books might be best in the library or family room, while computer magazines might go in a basket beside your lounge chair to read during commercials. Millions of us enjoy reading in the bathroom, so a magazine rack hanging on the back of the bathroom door might be the perfect place for the lightweight reading!

Alternative Measures

If bookshelf space is a problem, and you have eliminated all the publications you can, then what? If you have some books which are important to the family, but not particularly to you, identify your alternatives. Is there someone else in the family who would enjoy them more? If your children want them but are not in a position to take them now, put them in boxes in a safe, but less accessible location in your home—clearly labeled! If there is not any available space, consider one of the self storage units.

If you have books that are valuable to someone, but not to you or your family, donate them to a library or professional association, or sell them at a secondhand bookstore. Check your yellow pages to find a book dealer who will actually come to your house, so you can avoid the hassle of carting them around.

Consider alternatives to reading. There is nothing which says you are un-American if you don't read the daily newspaper. A friend of mine says it took him years to admit that he really could read all he wanted to of the newspaper by looking over the shoulder of the person standing next to him on the subway! There are also newstapes which give summaries of news stories. Although at first you may think the cost is astronomical, consider the money you will save on subscriptions and the time you will save on reading— particularly if in the past you have been piling the newspapers up instead of reading them anyway!

Books on tape are a great way to relax or to educate yourself while commuting. I carry a small portable tape recorder in the car, so if something comes up on the tape that I want to act upon, or make a note of, I can record it. This method helps avoid creating a tape pile, because you know there is something on it you want, just as noting the page number on the front of the magazine will make it easier to tear out the article that interested you so that you can throw the magazine away.

A client of mine used to have all kinds of books, magazines, and newspapers all over her house, until she built a new house and discovered what it cost her per square foot. When she saw what her packrat be- havior was costing her, she threw them all out! Keep in mind that this country is full of libraries.

17

Your "To Write" Pile

IF YOU WANT to see guilt written all over the faces of a lot of people in a big hurry, just mention the word "letter writing!" The mobility of our society and our changing lifestyles have created an enormous network of people with whom we would like, or think we ought, to communicate. The higher divorce and remarriage rates result in larger, extended families. More women in the workplace result in contact with many more people. This same changing lifestyle has complicated our lives and made it even more difficult to keep up our written communication.

Personal Correspondence

As with every other aspect of paper management that we have discussed, the step in solving this paper problem is selectivity. There will always be more people to write to than you will have time for, so choose those people who mean the most to you. Keep in mind that circumstances change, and we do outgrow friendships. At twenty-five you may have felt that your

Writing Letters Can Be Burdensome to Certain People.

college roommate would always be an important relationship in you life, but now you realize that your paths have led in different directions, and there is little you have in common.

Do whatever you can to make letter writing enjoyable and efficient. Choose stationery and a pen that you like and find easy to use. Select different styles of writing paper for different occasions. Carry notepaper in your handbag or briefcase so you can jot a quick note while you are waiting for an appointment. This is also a great way to use postcards that you pick up while on vacation.

Thank you notes and letters of condolence are a major concern in the area of correspondence. Not only do we want to do what is socially correct, but we want people to know that we appreciate their kindnesses and we care about their suffering. In some cases, you may find that it is easier for you to make a telephone call than it is to write a letter. If you feel you must write a letter, do whatever you can to simplify the process. I find it helpful to purchase multiple copies of any thank you or sympathy card I particularly like. Or, if you don't have a card on hand, and don't have time to get one, write a note on personal stationery.

Many times we put off writing a letter because there are so many things we want to say. The longer we put it off, the more there is to write. Then we decide we will wait until Christmas, but the holidays come and go, and the Christmas cards which we did manage to purchase are still in the desk drawer. Finally, we are so embarrassed by our negligence that we lose contact entirely. If you recognize that scenario, ask yourself when was the last time you got a short note from a friend and said, "My, that sure was a short note!" A short note is better than no note at all. Beware of perfectionism. Write what you can when you can, and the people who are truly friends will understand and be glad.

Birthdays and Anniversaries

There are a variety of ways to handle those annual special events. First of all, find a place to consistently list birthdays and anniversaries—special occasion book, a section of your "To Do" book or on a card in your Rolodex (one card for each month, if you keep track of many dates).

Then the question becomes how do you remind yourself to look at the list? One person I know looks at the list at the beginning of each month, and transfers into her calendar the day she needs to mail the card or gift (not the day of the birthday, when it is frequently too late to take action). You may prefer to do the entire year at once.

One of the hazards of purchasing greeting cards that you see and like, even if you don't know to whom you will send them, is the risk of forgetting you have them, or not being able to find them at the right time. To avoid this situation, establish a specific place to keep your greeting cards. Be sure that it is easily accessible if you want to encourage yourself to use them! If you keep more than twelve or fifteen cards on hand, organizing them by occasion will save you time and prevent frustration. Use large envelopes (8½" x 11½"), tuck in the flap to make a large pocket envelope, and write "Anniversary," "Birthday," etc. on the outside. Arrange them alphabetically.

Business vs. Pleasure

Again, it is very helpful to have on hand stationery which you can use for writing or typing business letters. Oftentimes, however, you can answer a business letter by writing a note on the letter itself (and keeping a copy for yourself only if necessary, rather than out of habit!). Another quick way to write a business letter is a postcard. I had some personalized ones printed to use for requesting information or confirming appointments.

Separate your "To Write" category into "Business" and "Personal." You may feel in the mood to write a quick thank you note, but not to inquire about a discrepancy in your credit card bill. Sometimes you may find it convenient, or even fun, to take a box of note stationery and your "To Write—Personal" file with you to the doctor's office or the beach.

Finally, if you are serious about keeping up with your friends through letters, set aside a regular time to do it, such as one Sunday per month, or one letter before your favorite Thursday night television program. And, remember, write just one letter a week, and you can communicate with 52 friends this year!

18

The Kitchen Papers

IN MANY IF not most homes, the kitchen or eating area is the "heart" of the home. It's easy to see how it can become a catchall for a multitude of paper.

How many times a week do you try to get dinner on the table and discover it piled deep in papers—the newspaper leftover from your morning coffee, the school papers your children brought home, the mail you grabbed out of the mailbox as you raced in the door (now sorted in several unidentified piles!), the insurance forms your spouse brought home from the office, and the gasoline credit card receipt you picked up from the car seat. Without a doubt, one of the major places we accumulate paper in our homes is in the kitchen. What can you do about it?

Kitchen Catch-All

The first step is to create a gathering place to put all the paper when you need to use the table, but don't have time to put away. It could be a large basket, a shelf, or a tray. The key to success in kitchen paper

management is to make an appointment with your-self to get back to the pile before it becomes too over-whelming, to separate what should come out of the catchall from what really *belongs* in the kitchen. You may find it helpful to do it on a regular basis—every Thursday night before your favorite television show, or once a month when you pay bills. Make an effort to keep the pile as small as possible by putting things away whenever you can. For example, if, as you pick up the mail, you see several pieces of "junk mail," throw them away immediately. It will also be much easier to keep the papers in the kitchen at a minimum if you have specific places for papers to go—for ex-ample, unread newspapers under the coffee table in the family room; read newspapers on the floor in the front hall closet, if you save them for the Scout drive, and directly in the wastebasket if you don't.

If your work center is in the kitchen, put the papers you need to act on in your "To Sort" tray until you are ready to take action on them. If your work center is in another room, take your paper there whether it is an office, your family room, bedroom or basement. Put the papers that belong to other family members in places designated for their attention.

Message Mania

One of the annoying results of our telephone-laden world is a myriad of notes—some written to us by others who have taken our telephone messages, and some written by us to ourselves as we talk on the telephone, or plan to talk on the telephone. What can you do to avoid, or at least minimize, this problem? How many times a week do you find a piece of paper with notes from several different telephone conversations? The major question is, "Where do I put it?" One very simple solution is to get a smaller size notepad by the phone—I like 5" x 7"—and use one piece of paper, or more if necessary, for each telephone call. Then at the end of the conversation, you can ask the question, "What is the next action required on this piece of paper?" The answer will tell you where to put it. (For more details on this process, see Chapter 9.) In many instances, all you need to do is double check to see that the number is in your telephone number system, and then you can throw away one more piece of paper.

Be sure to designate a place where family members can check to see if they have telephone messages. You can use a bulletin board, a plastic message holder, magnets on the refrigerator, or envelopes attached to the wall or a door. Be sure the owner's names are clearly labeled so there is no confusion! Encourage family members to note on the message the date and time they took the call.

One of the major factors in organizing the papers

related to your telephone is actually returning the calls. All the organization in the world will not make the papers go away. Only you, or someone to whom you delegate, can do that. With that in mind, a few time management tips with regard to telephone calls are in order. *Find one place to put all the papers that require telephone calls.* Put them in a file folder with a label "Call", in a pile near your telephone, or make a list of the people you need to call. It will take less time to make the calls if you put the phone numbers on the list as well. Then when you have time to make one phone call, it will not require much more time to make two or three. Try to group calls together whenever possible, and be selective in the time you choose. If you call the same people frequently, and they are often difficult to reach, ask them for guidelines about when is a good time to talk with them. If you call someone and get their answering machine, leave as complete a message as possible. Include why you called, whether you expect them to return the call, and if so, what is the best time to call.

Speaking of answering machines, whether you like them or not, they are a fact in our society, so it is in your best interest to accept them, and to learn to use them to your advantage. And you will never again have to accept "I tried to call you, but you were never home!" You will discover that they can do amazing things! I now have a machine that answers two telephone lines with separate messages. I can determine which line will be answered by machine and can even change the message when I am away from my home. I call home and by pushing one number, the machine will tell me how many calls I have received. Then it plays each of the messages and tells me which line the call came in on, and at what time. At the end of the message, the machine tells me what to do if I want

to erase the messages, save the messages, or change my message. The machine also has a "memo" capability, so that if my children want to give me a message but do not know where I am, or don't feel like writing it down, they can talk into the machine and it will record their message! That machine has simplified my life more than any kitchen appliance I every purchased (my heart nearly stopped one day when I walked in the door to get my messages and the machine announced, "I detect a malfunction. Please check your message!" Amazing!).

People frequently complain about making phone calls because they end up spending so much time on the telephone. There are several precautionary measures you can take when making a phone call. First identify yourself and why you are calling. For example, "Hi,

Jerry. This is Pat Roberts. I am calling to find out what time our Community Association meeting is on Friday." If your call is a complicated one, and involves several issues, make an agenda for yourself so you can check items off as you discuss them. (Use your "To Do" Book. See Chapter 7.) If you are afraid you will not get all the issues covered, prioritize them and be sure to start with the most important. At the end of the call, decide when you will call again, or what other way you could get the information you need. If you are frustrated by calls from other people, learn to take control of your time. Use an answering machine so you can control when you take calls. Use assertive language such as, "What can I do for you?" Be honest! "I promised myself I would do something with my desk today, and I've got to get going."

Kitchen Transitions

Obviously some papers belong in the kitchen—recipes, cookbooks, entertainment records, coupons (if you are a user, and not just a collector), and take-out menus.

It is important to recognize that your attitude toward the kitchen, and toward cooking, will determine to a great extent how your kitchen should be organized. There are many factors that contribute to our feelings, and it is also important to acknowledge that our feelings change with time and circumstances. This does not mean that we are being lazy or negligent, just that our priorities have changed.

Frequently I find clients who are overwhelmed with guilt, and with piles of papers in the kitchen, because they are afraid to admit that they are not as interested in cooking as they once were. I am a good example. When I was first married, my husband and I entertained often. We had three children and we were on a limited budget. For all of these reasons, I spent a considerable amount of time with papers in the kitchen—collecting coupons, selecting recipes, keeping records of what I served guests, educating myself about the nutritional needs of my children, and reading the food columns in the newspapers.

When I got a divorce, after 14 years of marriage, my feelings about the kitchen changed drastically. Because my children were with me only part time, I ate out often. If fact, for the first several months, I could scarcely stand to go into a grocery store, let alone read the food columns, because I associated those activities with the family life I missed. I spent the energy previously spent in the kitchen on my career. Then I married a man who has two children.

Now there are five teenagers in and out of our home, and the organization needs in the kitchen have changed drastically. Because family members—and their friends—are in and out frequently, it is important to have lots of food possibilities at a moment's notice. I am once again interested in recipes, but very different ones from those that interested me 15 years ago. For example, I used to believe that if I didn't spend at least an hour preparing the evening meal, no compliment was justified. Now I look for ten-minute recipes that generate smiles—or at least fill stomachs! In addition, most of my cooking now is done in the microwave. Since we rarely have a "sit-down meal," I make individual meals that can be reheated easily in the microwave. Entertaining now is much more informal, so souffles that have to be eaten the moment they come out of the oven are of little interest. Dishes that can be prepared in advance of the event are essential.

Designing Your Cookbook and Recipe System

Let's take a look at the issue of recipes and cook-books. First of all, accept the fact that you may not organize your recipes and cookbooks the same way your mother did! That does not mean you are wrong—just different, because your lifestyle, priorities and needs are different from those of your mother. So erase from your mind those "shoulds" and think about what you need to make a system work for you. If you think about it, you will probably recognize that most of your cooking is done from less than 20% of your recipes. It is my observation that the axiom "less is more" is certainly true in the kitchen. The more recipes people have, the fewer they use. Often we spend more time agonizing over the fact we don't use them, or beating ourselves because we haven't organized them, than we do cooking them! The only solution is to put a stop to this negative cycle.

One common pitfall is to wait to set up a system for today's recipes until you have conquered the backlog of recipes. It will be easier to set up a system for the recipes you are collecting now. Then incorporate the backlog into the new system as you have the time, energy, and interest.

There are dozens of systems on the market for organizing recipes. If you have found one that suits your needs, by all means use it. In my experience, many of them do not allow for the flexibility that is essential in creating a system that is workable for your particular situation. For example, the categories may not be the same as you would use, or the space allowed to write, type, or glue the recipe not large enough.

Keep in mind that this is not a place to let your

perfectionism get in the way of starting the task! The system does not need to be perfect, and probably will not be. You can always make adjustments as you experiment.

One of the easiest ways to get started is with manila folders, so you can sort your recipes into categories. Designate a place, preferably in or near the kitchen, where you will keep recipes. Put all the supplies you will need there: manila file folders, felt tip pen to label the files, scissors, scotch tape, index cards, recipe cards, blank recipe book or whatever system you plan to use.

Your Recipe Categories

There are dozens of ways to categorize recipes—just compare cookbook indexes, if you doubt it—so don't waste energy agonizing over what categories you want to use. Instead of trying to think up the categories first, start with the recipes you have. Ask yourself, "If I were looking for this recipe, what would I think of?" As a general rule, start with broader categories first, such as "Bread." Then if the quantity of recipes in that category becomes too bulky to manage, you can subdivide it into "Yeast Breads," "Muffins," Sweet Breads," etc. If you spend a great deal of time cooking, entertaining, and enjoy spending time planning menus, testing new recipes, etc., then you may want your categories to be very specific from the start. However, most people find it simpler if they use more general categories.

I find it helpful to separate the "tried and true" recipes from those I would like to try. When I am convinced a recipe is a "winner", and I don't keep it unless it is, I put it on a 4" x 6" index card and into a card box. The box is divided into categories the same way I divided the recipes in the manila file folders.

The recipes I would like to try stay in the manila file folders divided by categories. It is not necessary to type or handwrite the recipe, unless you particularly want to. The fastest way is to "cut and paste" the recipe to fit on the index card. You may wish to make notes on the card about when you served it, what you served with it, or suggestions for adaptations of the recipe.

Decide whether to separate your microwave recipes from your conventional recipes. Of course, many conventional recipes can be adapted to microwave, but many people think of them quite separately.

Your Recipe Index

If you are frequently frustrated because you can't find a recipe from one of your many cookbooks that you used successfully on a previous occasion, create a recipe index. The simplest way is to take a loose-leaf notebook, and divide it into the same categories you used when you sorted your recipes. List the name of the recipe, the name of the cookbook, and the page number in your index under the appropriate category. The added advantage of this system is that it is very helpful in meal planning. If, for example, you have everything you need for a meal except a salad, you can quickly check the "Salad" category in your recipe index for ideas about what would fit in your menu.

Conquering the Recipe Backlog

Once you have a recipe system set up and working, you can decide whether you want to tackle the backlog. You may decide it makes more sense to toss the entire collection!

The first step in conquering any backlog is to make an appointment with yourself to do it. The length of the appointment will depend on your working style. You will enjoy this project, and want to spend a long time on it? Is it a frustrating project, and you will have a limited attention span? Do circumstances dictate that it will be done on a piecemeal basis, even though you would prefer to spend more time at it? Once you have made that decision, write down the commitment to yourself on your calendar.

Is there a family member or friend who will help you? If so, get them involved in the appointment so you will be less likely to ignore it. If it is a major problem for you, hire a professional—"Yes, Virginia, there are people who are good enough, and like it enough, to get paid for organizing recipes."

The second step in conquering the backlog is to determine where you will do it. If at all possible, set up a place you can use until the project is completed. (I declared the dining room off limits to the family for two weeks, and did it there.) Or, set up a card table in the corner of a room somewhere. It will be much easier, and less frustrating, if you don't have to get everything out each time you want to work—and you may find that you will work a few minutes here and there, unplanned, if everything is accessible. My telephone cord stretches into my dining room, so I found I could talk on the phone and organize recipes at the same time.

The next step is to collect all the recipes you have, or part of them, if looking at them all is too overwhelming! Undoubtedly along the way you will get discouraged and overwhelmed. Keep asking yourself questions:

(1) Do I really need this?

(2) Does this recipe exist somewhere else?

(3) How long has it been since I've used, or had, this recipe?

(4) What is the worst possible thing that would happen if I tossed it?

Trying New Recipes

You may well discover that your standards change as you recognize how much work is involved to keep everything you had planned to keep! One of the essential steps in keeping the recipes in your kitchen under control is developing a method of trying new ones. Whenever I begin to feel like I am in a cooking rut, or if I have some extra time, I choose six to eight recipes I would like to try in the next few weeks. Usually I pick one or two main dishes, one or two salads or vegetables, one or two soups, and one or two desserts.

The next step is the important one. Take time when you are selecting your recipes to make a note on your shopping list of the ingredients you will need to prepare these dishes. Finally, clip the recipes to a magnet on the refrigerator, or put them in a special compartment in your recipe box or book. Then when you are rushed to get dinner on the table, but want to try something new, you will have the menu idea and the ingredients right at your finger tips. (The same technique can be used in choosing recipes that your children can prepare if they cook while you are working).

The final step in this system is making a decision about the recipe after you have eaten the results. Was it great? If not, why keep it? Avoid the "I really should give it one more try" syndrome. There are undoubtedly thousands more you can try which might be, and there is no shortage of recipes, so let it go! Then your recipe collection becomes something you really treasure instead of tolerate.

One winter I was snowbound for four days. I had a wonderful time experimenting with my new recipes. In addition, I had a freezer full of food which could be microwaved for a speedy nutritious meal on the days following the snow when I was too busy catching up on lost time to spend time cooking.

Entertainment Records

A client of mine had invited a certain gentleman to her home on several occasions with various dinner guests. She was most embarrassed to discover that she had served tomatoes stuffed with spinach on the last three occasions! (Unfortunately, he didn't like it the first time!)

One way to avoid that problem is to create a notebook to record your entertaining. Just as with the recipes, there are various ways to organize it. If you entertain lavishly and frequently have the same guests, it will require more time to maintain the system than if you entertain simply and/or infrequently. The simplest way is to list the events in chronological order. Include the menu, table decorations, guest list (and seating arrangement, if you wish), and perhaps even what you wore. It is also helpful to list suggestions you have on any improvements you might want to make when you entertain again, whether it is a slight change in a recipe (which should be noted on your recipe card or in your recipe book), a suggestion about serving logistics (for example, the coffee should be on a separate table or serve small forks with the appetizers), or a note about the flowers.

If you entertain frequently, and are particularly

concerned about not duplicating menus for the same guests, you could put a separate alphabetical section in your book. Each guest would have a small section where you could put the date on which you entertained him/her. Then you could check the chronological list for the menu that guest was served. For example, under "A", you would have: "Adams, John—3/6/86; 6/7/87; 10/2/87; 5/4/88; etc. You could also note there any items of concern when entertaining that guest—allergies, food preferences, medical concerns, etc.

To Market, To Market

A major issue is keeping track of the food we have on hand and the food we need to purchase. We find it helpful to have a shopping list posted on the refrigerator, with a pencil permanently attached to a string!

There are also paper management techniques you can use to simplify your shopping trips. For example, if you do the majority of your shopping in the same store, you may find it time-effective to create a checklist of the items you most frequently purchase, arranged in the order of the grocery store aisles. Leave space in each section for special items which are not regularly on your list.

Make a dozen copies. After you have tried the system that many times, you can probably identify ways you want to change the form. You may decide to post the form itself on the refrigerator door to check off items as you go, or, if there are family members who are unable or unwilling to use the list, it may be easier to transfer the ad hoc list from the refrigerator onto the form just before you go to the store.

If you have problems with people forgetting to put items on the list when they use the last of something, try making a list of commonly used items in your kitchen. Then, just before you do a major shopping, you can make a quick check in the kitchen to see which of those items are low in supply.

Coupon Coordination

A discussion of papers in the kitchen would not be complete without including the issue of coupons. Decision-making and organization, in that order, are the keys to saving with manufacturers coupons and refund offers.

The first decision to make is whether you are really serious or committed to the idea of coupon clipping. My personal opinion is that unless you enjoy doing it, or your budget requires it, coupon saving is too much trouble. Ask yourself, "Do I really save money when I consider the time it takes me? Do I end up buying more expensive products that I would not necessarily buy if I did not have the coupon? Is clipping coupons an attempt to assuage my guilt feelings over excess spending habits, or an effort to appease my mother?" One man I know looks on it as a game, and uses it for relaxation.

Many people I know clip only coupons worth 35 cents or more, and only for those products they routinely buy, such as coffee, laundry soap, and paper products. Other people spend two to three hours per week, and can save $30–50 per week on grocery purchases, in addition to the amount received in cash from rebate offers. I read in a newspaper about one woman who bought $113.05 worth of groceries for $1.69. The real price: Her office is a corner of the basement, where she has organized coupons, labels and proofs of purchases into 14 grocery bags, six cardboard boxes, eight filing cabinet drawers and a bookcase! "This kind of couponing is available to anyone who is willing to get organized," she said, peering over the mountain of groceries in her cart.

In order to organize coupons, the basic principle, "put like things together," certainly applies. Establish categories for your coupons in the same way you establish categories for your recipes. Ask the question, "If I wanted this coupon, what category would I think of?"

There are several possibilities for categories, such as "Paper Products," "Cleaning Products," and "Vegetables" (this could be broken down in "Vegetables—Frozen," and "Vegetables—Canned"). In addition, you may want a separate system for refunds. It could be located in the same container, but in a separate section. Within that system, you would have the same categories as you had for coupons. In addition, you may want a section for "Refunds in Progress."

Keep a supply of return address labels, envelopes, and stamps on hand. For those refund offers which require several proof of purchase labels, put the pre-addressed envelope with the expiration date on the top right-hand corner of the envelope.

The techniques you use for storing coupons is also important. Decide whether you will always carry all your coupons with you when you go to the store, or whether you will have a "Master Coupon Box" at home from which you can pull out those coupons you want to take with you to the store. While at the store, you may use a regular business size envelope, or several, or you may purchase a "Coupon Billfold" designed specifically for that purpose. It is unlikely that the categories in a pre-designed system will be the same as yours, so feel free to put on your own labels to make the system work for you.

One woman I know divides her coupons according to the shopping aisles in her local store. Not only does the system add continuity to her coupon and refund hobby, but it saves her an incredible amount of time. Be sure you purge coupons on a regular basis.

Experiment until you find a method that works for you. There is not a right or wrong decision on this issue. Just decide, recognizing that you can change your decision at any time, based on your current circumstances. Once your decision is made, then concentrate on setting up the system needed to make your decision workable. But above all, create a system that gives you a feeling of success!

19

Children and Paper

CHILDREN AND PAPER are synonymous in our society. As soon as a woman even begins to think about starting a family, the paper begins to accumulate—articles on overcoming fertility problems, information on childbirth classes, advertisements from childcare services, notices of "mother's day out" programs, descriptions of childrearing techniques, and books about the psychological impact of parenting and the "how to's" of surviving parenthood.

There are numerous approaches to surviving this paper blizzard, but the first and most important step is to start some kind of system. As your children grow older, the system will need to change, but you don't need to worry about that now.

For the Mother-to-Be

The first step toward establishing a system that will work for you is to examine your own feelings about keeping and using information. Is it important to you to have easy access to articles about childrearing, or

Sasha

Perhaps Your Child Could Benefit from Paper Management, too...

would you be more likely to ask your doctor, a phychologist, or discuss it with your mother or a friend? Do you need the information near you to feel secure, even if you never need it? Or does having paper around create additional stress, guilt, or frustration? Is it realistic that you will take the time and effort required to maintain an extensive library, or is there someone else in the family who will help you? These are important questions to answer to prevent setting unrealistic standards for yourself. You create a "no-win" situation if you feel guilty because you keep too much, and feel guilty if you don't! Eliminate the "shoulds," and acknowledge what will work for you.

Collect and Categorize

The simplest way to begin any system is to collect all the information you have into the largest general category. In this case, "CHILDREN." Find a container, a basket, shelf, or file and label it clearly. If there is more information than can be easily handled and the file becomes too bulky, the next step is to divide the information into the next logical categories. For example, information about children can be categorized into areas of concern such as education, medical, memorabilia, legal information, and toys and equipment. Notice that "toys and equipment" are put together, because it is frequently too difficult to differentiate between the two categories. However, you may have "TOYS AND EQUIPMENT—Owned" and "TOYS AND EQUIPMENT—Shopping Information."

One of the facts about paper management is that our needs are constantly changing. A system that works when a child is six months old might be totally inappropriate when she is sixteen, and the system which works when she is sixteen will be overkill when she is thirty-six. For example, when your child is in elementary school, a file labeled "EDUCATION" may be sufficient. However, when he enters high school, that category may be too general. The categories you will need at this point depend on your particular style and on your child's interests. If you are very active in your educational program, you may need a file for "PTA," "COLLEGE PREPARATION," or "EXTRACURRICULAR ACTIVITIES." "EXTRACURRICULAR ACTIVITIES" may need to be subdivided into "GYMNASTICS," "BOY SCOUTS," etc.

If you want to keep all your files about your child together, put the child's name at the beginning of each label: "SUSAN—Education," "SUSAN—Sports," for example.

If you know that you will not take the time to develop a finite system, find a basket, shelf, or file and label it "JOHN—Education." It may take you ten minutes to go through the entire box if you need a copy of an Award Certificate to go with a college application, but it will be a massive improvement over having all the members of the family turning the house upside down looking for that large brown envelope!

As I have discussed previously, it is important to revise any system to meet the current needs. Setting up a system for children and paper is a good example. If your child is very young, one file folder labeled "JOHN" will probably be enough. As John grows, however, you will need to expand the system. In elementary school, for example, you will probably need only one file for educational information. However, as he begins to make plans for college, you may want several. As the years go by, and he becomes more independent, you may discover that one folder labeled "JOHN" will once again be sufficient. At this point all the report cards for kindergarten through high school become highly irrelevant. Choose one or two for your grandchildren to see.

Teach Your Children Well

With all the obligations and options in today's world, it is very easy for a parent to spend an inordinate amount of time being a social secretary, or just a "nagger." Teaching your child organization skills will benefit you and your child—for life!

One of the biggest problems that adults face in the complicated world in which we now live is making choices. Over and over I find houses buried in paper because adults feel compelled to do it all—read every book, newspaper and magazine, keep every photo and memento, or go to every concert, seminar, and reception. Living a happy and healthy life, or even just coping, in today's world means making choices. Remember, *clutter is postponed decisions*. As parents we have an obligation to teach that concept to our children, and one place to begin is with paper.

There are many steps you can take to help your children learn how to manage the paper in their lives, as well as to become good time managers.

As soon as Jenny begins to go to any organized playgroup or educational program, you will begin to accumulate paper. Designate a special place for her to put the papers she brings home from school. If you start this habit early, you will avoid many panic situations of trying to find a trip permission slip when you should be getting ready for work or running out the door to catch the car pool. Each evening or first thing in the morning you can check and see what came home from school, and what requires your attention.

The Art Pile

One of the major issues in the years to come will be the creative papers your child brings home. Young children produce enough paper to fill a small art gallery within a week. The big question is which of these 400 finger-painted gems will become cherished examples of the early works of upcoming Picassos. There is nothing wrong with keeping everything that our children create if we have plenty of space to keep it, and plenty of energy to organize it. But few people have either. It is easy to get caught in the trap of feeling guilty if we throw away the things our children make, and feeling overwhelmed if we don't. I think it is essential to involve your children in the selection process from the beginning.

You can use this process as a tool for teaching them decision making techniques, which will be important to know in the years to come. All the papers which you would like to keep can be put in a basket, or on a bulletin board with your child's name prominently displayed. Then when the basket gets full, or the bulletin board gets crowded, encourage Susan to choose her three favorite papers, which can be put in a Memorabilia Box for safe keeping. Put the child's name, age, and date on the back to make it more meaningful 20 years from now.

There are other creative uses for artwork as well. Put several creations together and make a collage for your child's wall or to use as a present for a relative. Grandparents, aunts and uncles are delighted to receive letters from children. Have your child write a short message on the back of the painting or just send the painting—signed, of course! Teach your child the value of recycling. Artwork makes wonderful wrapping paper for gifts to take to birthday parties.

Kids and Calendars

As your children get older, there are many other steps you can take to help them learn how to manage the paper in their lives, and to improve their time management skills. For example, put a large calendar with plenty of writing space in an easily accessible place. The refrigerator is frequently a good choice, because everyone ends up there sooner or later! Have each child note when he or she needs transportation to basketball, cookies for a school party, or plans to spend the night at a friend's house. This method helps you plan your schedule and avoids last-minute crises. If

Sam comes running to you at the last minute and says, "Mom, I need a ride to gymnastics," you can say, "I didn't see it on the calendar, Son, and I can't take you right now." If he misses an important practice, or is late for his game, it won't take him long to realize that he has to take some responsibility for his own life. Obviously, you have to take into account unusual circumstances and make exceptions when you feel it is appropriate to do so.

Don't forget that you owe the same courtesy to your children. For the career parent, this is a great place to communicate facts about your schedule that will affect your son or daughter. Include travel schedules, night meetings, or houseguests. Consider using different colored pens for each member of the family, and be sure to attach the pens on a long string next to the calendar so you won't hear the excuse "I couldn't find a pencil!"

As soon as Johnny begins getting school assignments in advance, help him choose an assignment book. Teach him how to plot out complicated assignments on a calendar. If there are ten chapters in the book and twenty days until the assignment is due, it means reading one-half chapter each day—or does it work better to read two chapters at a time, and choose those days on which there are not other obligations such as piano lessons or soccer practice. Discuss the concept of choosing styles. Remind him to watch for family commitments that might affect his schedule. Recognize that his style may not be the same as yours, but that does not mean it is wrong.

Encourage your children to use a calendar for keeping track of sports events, babysitting commitments, job responsibilities at home, birthdays they want to remember, etc.

The calendar is also an excellent place to help your

child understand the importance of goal setting. If, for example, Suzanne really, really wants to take a trip this summer which you feel is too expensive, or you feel she should contribute to the cost, help her plan how she could make it happen by using the calendar. Count the number of weeks until she needs the money, and determine how much money she will have to make every week if she is to succeed. She can use the calendar to block out time when she will work, and set goals for raising the money.

Your Child's Own Files

As your child gets older, help him or her to organize the papers he or she needs to cope with daily life. Purchase several file folders and help label them according to his or her needs. Make a category for each subject at school and each area of interest. At the end of the year encourage and assist your child, if necessary, in cleaning out the file and determining what papers he or she would like to keep as mementos, and which have served their purpose and can be thrown away.

If your children are involved in several organizations, a file called "DIRECTORIES" can be very useful to keep the lists of participant's names that you receive from Scouts, sports, school, youth group, etc. This file can save many hassles when Saturday morning rolls around, and you are madly trying to find a ride to soccer for your child. The information is also helpful if they are sending out party invitations or trying to locate a friend's phone number or address.

My 15-year-old son stopped in my office one day and noticed on my desk an X-Rack—a plastic frame designed to hold hanging file folders. He's a "gadget lover", and interested in art. He asked if I would get him one. The combination of the uniqueness of the file holder, and the bright-colored file folders with plastic tabs fascinated him, and gave me a terrific opening to help him in setting up a file system for his needs. It is very important to do whatever you can to make the organizing process appeal to your child. It's a great way to create one-on-one time, and you benefit doubly because both you and your child's lives will run more smoothly.

Your child may also want files that relate to special interests. For example, your teenager might want a category on "FASHION" or "SHOPPING IDEAS" to take on your next shopping trip.

Be sure to make a file index, or list of the files, to keep in the very front of the files. The file index of a 19-year-old friend of mine looks like this:

Jeff's Files

*Car
 Carnegie Melon—General
 Carnegie Melon—Courses, grades, loan
 Computer Languages
*Employment—Paycheck stuff, rules
 Fantasy Games
 Finance—Bank account, cancelled checks
 Harvard
 Legal Stuff—Leases/credit card info
*Medical
 NASA
 Northern Virginia Community College
 Resume
 Stories
 Taxes
 Utilities
 Writing/Papers

*These files he takes home for the summer.

This same friend told me he started at age ten with two files: stories and miscellaneous.

Failure to Communicate

One area which can be a constant frustration in families is communication, particularly in the home where there is a single parent, or both parents are working. Mom races in the door after being caught in a traffic jam and spending the last hour concerned that Sally was OK, only to discover that Sally is nowhere to be seen! Or Dad goes upstairs to bed at 11:00 p.m. and finds a message on the pad beside the phone which tells him to call an important business colleague at 8:00 p.m. How can this situation be avoided? Designate a communication center that is convenient for everyone. Again, the refrigerator is usually a good place—or the kitchen table. Of course, it's also the place to put chore reminders, but be sure the messages are not always things to do. You can also use that tool to communicate non-essential, but very important messages, like "Hope you had a good day at school. I love you. Mom"

20

Travel and Papers

A PRIMARY EXAMPLE of how paperwork has multiplied in our modern world is found in the area of travel: Bonus programs for airline travel, car rentals and hotel accommodations. Entire books have been written, newletters published and computer software designed to make it easier for the traveler to take advantage of all of these offers. Not taking advantage of such offers creates the same kind of emotion in us as not submitting our medical expenses to the insurance company for reimbursement!

Sasha

All That Paraphernalia

Travel brings with it other kinds of paper problems as well: maps, directions, confirmations, tickets, itineraries, notes about people to see and things to do, papers we need to take with us on the trip, addresses and phone numbers, traveler's checks, passports, and all the identification cards with numbers you need in order to get credit for those fabulous bonus programs.

Then there are all the papers you collect while you are traveling: more maps, phone numbers, and addresses of favorite restaurants and shops, new friends made, receipts for purchases which are being shipped to you, boarding passes and ticket stubs, travel brochures and a variety of memorabilia.

If your trip involved any meetings, you will undoubtedly have a pile of papers that contain all kinds of wonderful information you want to keep or use.

You arrive home from the trip with the best of intentions about going through all those papers, but as soon as you walk in the door, you are confronted with all the mail that arrived while you were away. So it is likely that the trip papers are pushed aside to deal with more pressing matters. After several weeks, you get tired of looking at them, or you have company coming and need to clear off the table, so into a drawer they go, never to be seen again!

Do you cut out travel articles? Collect travel magazines? Reviews about travel books? In order for them to be useful to you, you will need to organize them in some way. When was the last time you went through a pile of old magazines to find that article about the terrific restaurant in San Francisco?

Let's take a look at the various areas and see what

can be done to manage the paper in this area of our lives.

Essential Information

First of all, consider the travel information we want to keep for reference. This would include maps, travel brochures, information from past trips, newsletters from travel services and bonus programs information. The first step is to get all the information together. If you have a small amount, you may need something as simple as a file or box labeled "Travel Information." But if you have more than will fit into one category comfortably, then you need to decide how to organize the information. One way would be to organize it by category. For example, make a pile for maps, another for airline information, another for travel brochures, etc. These could then be incorporated into your filing system under "TRAVEL," so the labels would look like this: "TRAVEL—Airline Information," "TRAVEL—Brochures," "TRAVEL—Receipts," etc. For the frequent traveler this system will still need refining.

For example, if you participate in several frequent flyer programs, you will need a separate file for each airline, so you would have a series of files such as "AIRLINES—American," "AIRLINES—Continental," "AIRLINES—Pan-Am," "AIRLINES—TWA," etc. If your immediate reaction is horror at the thought of so many files, consider this. Suppose you are rushing out of the door to grab a flight. The last thing in the world you need to have to do is go through a pile of papers from an airline you are not taking. It will take only seconds to grab the information from the appropriate airline file. You may find it helpful to put them on your Rolodex, along with the phone numbers of the companies.

You will soon discover that your airline files can become very bulky very quickly, so it is important to establish your retention guidelines. I would suggest you keep your monthly statements for as long as you participate in the program, because airlines will sometimes offer special offers to travelers who have accumulated a certain number of miles during a certain length of time. Most airlines send a monthly newsletter. Keep only the latest one, unless there is specific information in an older newsletter. If so, identify clearly what information interests you so that you quickly identify why you kept that particular newsletter.

This same system will work for bonus programs for hotels and car rentals. Of course, the most important information to have is your membership number.

One of the other complicating factors in this issue are the "Tie-in Programs." For example, certain airlines have reciprocal privileges. Or, if you fly one airline and rent your car from a tie-in agency, you can get bonus miles. There are several books and newsletters on the market which describe these offers. If you are serious about collecting bonus points, one of them would be worth your investment.

Maps and Brochures

Maps are another example of a paper problem for the traveler. If you have only a dozen or so maps, one file or box will be plenty. But if you have more than that, refine your system by geographic area. I started with "U.S.—Northeast," "U.S.—Northwest,", U.S.—Southeast," "U.S.—Southwest." As my travel increased dramatically, I now have one file for every state, and several for foreign countries.

What about travel brochures? In order to determine how these should be filed, you need to identify why you are keeping them. Keep in mind that the answer might not be the same for each brochure. You may be keeping one strictly as a memento of a beautiful experience, another as a reference in case you return, or another to share with a friend. In order to determine what you should do with the brochure, ask yourself, *"Under what circumstances would I want this information?"* The answer will help you determine where you should file it. Put a date on the brochure when you file it, so it will be easier to clean out the files in the years to come.

If you or your family enjoy taking day trips, but sometimes have difficulty thinking of where to go on the spur of the moment, create a "DAY TRIP IDEAS" file. This can also be useful if you have long-term house guests you are trying to entertain! "Vacation Ideas" can also be a useful file when it is time for the family to decide on a summer vacation plan.

If you have more than 8 to 10 travel files, I suggest you create a separate filing system for travel, rather than incorporating them into your existing files. Identify travel files with a particular color so you can recognize them easily.

Before the Trip

As soon as you begin planning for any trip, make a file with the destination on the label, such as "NEW YORK." This will provide an immediate place to put any information regarding the trip—tickets, itinerary, reminders of things you want to take with you, contacts you want to make while you are there, or places you want to visit or shop. If you travel frequently, you may have several trip files at one time.

If you travel frequently, make a standard packing list. Keep it in your "To Do" Book or in your suitcase. Then as soon as you begin planning a trip, take a standard packing list and put it in the "New York Trip" file. As you think of things you want to take with you, note them on the packing list. As you pack your suitcase, check off each item, and note the specific number taken. For example, "Dress Shirts—6." If you are concerned about losing your luggage and being able to substantiate a claim, keep the list until you return from the trip. People who travel with children can use the list to help their children get everything repacked in the suitcase. (One client puts her list in a plastic folder, and then uses a grease pencil to check it off. Then it can be easily erased after each use.) When my daughter was twelve, she decided to take the list with her so that when she was repacking her suitcase, she could check it off to be sure she remembered to bring everything home with her.

Make a "Pre-trip Checklist" to remind you of last-minute tasks which are easy to forget:

Check thermostat
Turn off coffeepot
Stop newspaper
Arrange for plant and pet care

If you have filed your travel reference material by geographical area, it will be very easy to check that file for any additional information you might want on the trip. Sometimes I even take the file with me for airplane reading. Be sure to take a list of frequent flyer numbers. These could be listed in your "To Do" Book under "Travel" or "Numbers."

On the Trip

If you are going to attend any kind of meeting while you are on the trip, and will be collecting a number of papers, I suggest you create Action Files. It will be easier to make decisions about what you want to do with the papers as you acquire them than it will be to go back through the papers when you return home. Action files might include "Write," "File," "Hold." (See Chapter 9).

What about travel receipts? You cannot decide what to do with a receipt unless you identify why it is useful to you. Do you need it to prove a tax deductible expense? If so, it could go with other tax information for the year. (See Chapter 13.) Are you keeping it until the china that you purchased arrives safely? If so, it could go in a "To Hold" file (See Chapter 9.) When the china arrives, it could go in "Personal Property" in case you need it to substantiate an insurance claim.

After the Trip

When the trip is over, put your ticket stub and boarding passes in the airline file until you are certain your miles have been credited to your account. Then you can throw the boarding passes away. The ticket stub should be filed only if you need it for a specific reason—for example, a business reimbursement or a tax deductible expense. Seriously consider putting it in the wastebasket if you cannot identify why you will need the receipt in the future.

Take action on any papers you have brought home with you, or incorporate them into your existing Action Files.

Finally, be sure to purge the trip file itself. Throw

away any information which is no longer relevant, and file the remaining information into the appropriate file.

Suppose you meet someone on a trip who lives in another city you visit frequently, or hope to visit one day. Put their name and address with a note about where you met in that geographical file. Does all this sound like to much drudgery? It may be a lifesaver if you find yourself stranded in their city one day, or just a lot of fun if you get together and reminisce about all the fun you had on that Caribbean cruise!

21

Home Computers and Paper

THERE ARE MANY books on the subject of personal computers. This is not the place for a major discussion about them, but it would be foolish to write a book on paper management in this day and age without mentioning personal computers. They can, without a doubt, do many miraculous things to help us manage our lives more effectively. They will not, however, solve a paper management problem. In fact, a personal computer can complicate paper management considerably, because it becomes so easy to create more paper. For example, you write a letter or a report and print out a copy in order to edit it. When you have completed the editing and entered the changes in the computer, you print out another copy. Within minutes you have doubled the amount of paper in your life.

In the Beginning

Purchasing a computer is not a simple issue. I had one client who had spent four years of her life, and

Some People Love Computers Because They Can Cut Down on Paper Clutter.

four file drawers of her office, collecting information on how to buy a computer! (In the end, I should add, she hired a consultant to help her make the decision!) Obviously this is an extreme example, but few people decide on Tuesday that they are going to get a computer, and go out and buy one Wednesday—or even next week!

After you have made the decisions necessary to purchase a computer, you face the challenge of learning how to use it. This is becoming a simpler issue as computers become more "user friendly," but as with any other new equipment you purchase, it does require time. Therefore, it is important that you do not postpone managing the paperwork in your life until you "get it on computer," or the task may become an overwhelming one.

Too Many Printouts

The computer will not make decisions for you. For example, people who have computers with programs that print special reports, especially home account systems, often feel compelled to print out every report possible to ensure that they are getting the most out of their computer. What they often get is confused!

This is also a major reason that paper gets out of hand. The best approach is to print one of each report the first time or two you use a new program. Then study the reports and determine which ones are useful to you, and print only those. Keep in mind that any paper is of extremely limited value to you if you cannot identify specifically why you are keeping it. Ask yourself that familiar question, *"Under what circumstances would I use this information?"* This not only cuts down on the amount of paper, it also cuts down on the amount of confusion.

It is essential to set up schedules for purging computer reports, just as you purge your paper Reference Files. Consider purging detail type reports quarterly, and keeping only summary reports for long-term reference.

Storing computer reports in binders will make them easier to manage and to reference. The quality and price of binders vary. Use metal or plastic-coated metal, which will last longer than the plain plastic ones, and cost less in the long run.

Label the binder as to contents and date. This will speed up the purging process considerably, and will make them easier to access while they are still in use.

If your printer is set up so that you lose one sheet of paper each time you print, save that paper for single sheet applications or for scratch paper. You can take discarded computer reports to your printer and have it cut and padded into handy scratch pads for a small charge (and, of course, there is always the bottom of the bird cage)!

Make Your Computer Work For You

A computer can simplify many of your paper management tasks. The computer is an excellent tool for maintaining a File Index. If you always have easy access to the computer, you may not even want to print out a copy, but more often you will find it helpful to print out one copy to keep in front of your files, and one copy at your desk. You can make entries and deletions by hand, and then periodically update it on the computer.

There are software products you can use to replace or supplement your calendar, your Rolodex, and your "To Do" list. You can even organize your recipes. But before you take that step, be sure the results will be worth the time and energy it will take to enter the data in your computer and to maintain it. You may find that a $10 calendar or a $5 index card box for your recipes will do just as well. On the other hand, the "sort" capabilities of a computer can be a real boost to your Rolodex and eliminate the problem of whether to list Peter Pipewrench under "plumber," "household repairs," or "Pipewrench, Peter."

There are numerous software packages for managing your finances. It is important, however, that you know what information you need. If you couldn't decide what information to put in a budget book, a computer may not solve the problem.

22

Caging That Tiger!

AT THIS POINT, a review of the basic components of this paper management system is in order. Keep in mind that every piece of paper in your life can be categorized into one of seven categories:

"To Sort" Tray
Wastebasket
Calendar/s
"To Do" List
Rolodex/Phone Book
Action Files
Reference Files

Each time you find a pile of papers that need your decision-making, ask yourself these questions about each piece:

1. Can this go in the wastebasket?

2. If not, do I need to make an appointment with myself? If so, enter the information in your calendar.

3. Does this piece of paper require action or recall by me at some yet undetermined time in the future? If so, enter it in your "To Do" Book.

4. Are there any addresses, telephone numbers, or pieces of "mini information" that could go on your Rolodex?

5. If I have entered the information in any of the above places, do I still need to keep the piece of paper? If so, is it a paper that requires action or am I keeping it for reference?

6. If it requires action, what specific action do I need to take? The answer will tell you into which Action File you should put it.

7. If I am keeping it for reference, what word would I think of if I wanted this piece of paper again? The answer will tell you into what Reference File you should put it.

Getting Rid of the Boxes

In the question and answer period following one of my speeches a woman asked, "I have four large packing boxes full of papers that I have been telling myself for the past three years I will organize 'one of these days,' but each time I try I am totally overwhelmed. What can I do?"

I can think of only two options for getting rid of those boxes: (1) Decide that since you have survived for the past three years without using any of the information in those boxes, take a deep breath and toss them all in the trash, or (2) Go through the papers one by one using the system described in this book, making decisions on each one. In order to determine which option you want to choose, it may help you to know that going through the equivalent of one vertical file cabinet drawer will take approximately four hours. If the peace of mind you will get from going through the papers one by one is worth four hours of your time, by all means make an appointment with yourself to do it as soon as possible. If spending the four hours in some other way is more important to you, then throw the boxes away immediately. If you find yourself postponing the decision, ask yourself, "What am I going to know tomorrow that I don't know today?"

Just Get Started

At this point, one of the major questions you may have is "How long will it take?" You cannot expect to solve all of your paper management problems overnight. Do not worry about how long it will take. Just get started. One of the most exciting things you will discover is that what you learn in organizing one area of your life will carry over into other areas. As you enjoy your successes, you will be encouraged to keep going.

Keep It Growing

There are no magic wands! No matter how terrific the system you develop, it will not maintain itself, and it will not last forever. If after reading this book, or even parts of this book, you have to admit that you are not willing to do what needs to be done, then your assignment is to determine who will help you and how.

Keep in mind, however, that the key issue in any paper management system is decision making. You will either have to make the decisions yourself, or give the person to whom you delegate your paper management the authority to make those decisions. A successful system will probably require a combination of decision making and delegation.

Many times a client will call me because a system they have established is not working. Nine times out of ten, the problem is not that the system was bad, but that they have outgrown the system. Personal paper management is an ongoing process. It will need to change as you change. If your priorities, your support system, your space availability, or your family situation change, you may need to adjust your system to fit those changes.

Call for Action

If you have read this book and still don't know how to do it, or want additional support or assistance for your specific needs, check your local yellow pages under "Organizing Consultants" or "Personal Services" and find someone who specializes in setting up systems for paper management. You may also want to write NAPO (National Association for Professional Organizers, 5350 Wilshire Blvd., P.O. Box 36E02, Los Angeles, CA 90036).

Many people procrastinate about making an appointment with an Organizing Consultant. Often they are stuck with the "clean up before the maid comes" syndrome, or they are concerned about how to prepare for his/her arrival.

Put aside any worries about needing to justify your situation. The Organizing Consultant's role is to provide professional advice, not to make judgments. Ask yourself the questions: "Why did I make this appointment with an Organizing Consultant?" and "What do I want to change?"

It is not *necessary* to do anything, but *if* you feel a need to get started, here are some suggestions:

1. We're going to begin work immediately. Choose where you would like to begin—with today's mail or the attic.

2. Gather together any supplies you may have on hand which will be helpful in the organizing process—file folders, labels, marking pens, boxes, containers, wastebaskets, etc.
3. Put all like things together—banking information, photographs, magazines, etc.

Relax! If you feel unsure about where to begin, or what to do, your Organizing Consultant has the knowledge and experience to guide you in making that decision.

What Can You Expect From an Organizing Consultant?

The first step in developing a good working relationship with an Organizing Consultant is to have a realistic understanding of what you can and should expect.

1. Complete confidentiality.
2. Open discussion about the cost of services.
3. Appointments scheduled to meet your professional and/or personal needs.
4. An ability to apply the "principles of organization" to any profession.
5. Expertise and experience in the "principles of organization" applied to personal and professional life.
6. Creative and innovative problem solving.
7. A willingness to do whatever task needs to be done in the interest of achieving mutually determined goals.
8. Physical assistance, as well as verbal instruction. A willingness to do whatever you would do—including getting dirty!
9. Shopping assistance if you need or want it.

10. Assistance in finding another professional resource if it is appropriate or desirable.
11. Availability and a continued interest in your situation should you desire.

A Note of Caution

It is always easier to see what someone else needs to do than it is to see what we need to do. In teaching organizing skills to families, one of my key roles is to insure that family members concentrate on solving their own organizing problems, instead of on what other family members need to do. As you read this book, and experiment with developing new paper management systems for yourself, resist the urge to insist that other people join you. Many of the systems you develop will automatically make paper management easier for other people, but let them discover it for themselves!

Although you are at the end of this book, you are at the beginning of a new adventure in learning to control the paper in your life. Remember, "In every organizing process, things will get worse before they get better." Try to remain optimistic. Forgive yourself when you see the mistakes you have made in the past and move on. Feeling bad about yourself does not help anything. Be willing to ask for help when you need it, and reward yourself for each accomplishment along the way. Now grab that tiger by the tail! You are on your way to a personal paper management system that works for you!

APPENDIX: Guidelines For Records Retention

Although much study has gone into the preparation of this schedule, the retention periods shown are not intended as final authority. There are over 900 Federal and State regulations governing this subject. Check with your tax commissioner for the statutes of limitations for your state, as well as the regulations of government agencies pertaining to your business. Also, there may be very good reasons to keep records longer than legally required, if you wish them for historical or reference purposes. However, it is *crucial* that you identify the reason for keeping the records in order to avoid becoming buried in them. If you don't know you have it, or you can't find it, it is of *no* value to you!

Be sure to include in your retention program a timetable for transferring records from active files to inactive storage. (At the end of the year, the beginning of the year, or after you have filed your income tax returns are logical times to do this.) You may find that the least complicated method for keeping records is to put all records for a given year into a large envelope or box, and store them in chronological order. When you put in the latest year's records, take out the envelope for the sixth year prior. Keep only those few items which require longer retention as noted in the guidelines. Do not overlook the fact that you often have more than one copy of the same record.

The guidelines here are conservative. That is, you may well be able to keep records for a shorter time than stated. The statute of limitations for IRS audits is 3 years from the date of return. If you income-average, you will need records for 5 years. Statute of limitations is 6 years if you under-report income by 25% or more. (No limitation exists if fraud is suspected, or no return is filed.) Therefore, it is advisable to keep a copy of your return permanently, but 6 years is adequate for supporting documents. (The IRS generally keeps copy of your return for 6 years, and you can obtain a copy for a moderate fee.)

Bank Statements: 6 years (If you wish to absolutely minimize storage requirements, all cancelled checks for items not related to taxes, i.e. personal care, food purchases, cash, etc., can be eliminated as soon as your checkbook is reconciled to the bank statement.)

Bill of Purchase for Property: as long as you own the property.

Bill of Sale for Property: 6 years.

Car Records:

    Sales Contract: as long as you own the car.

    Maintenance receipts: as long as you own the car for major repairs; others 1 yr. to cover possible parts warranty.

    Repair Estimates: 6 months.

Credit Card Statements: 6 years if they include tax deductible expenses, or 1 year for record of interest paid. Then put year-end statement into tax info for that year.

Dividend Payment Records: until annual dividend statement is supplied by the company. Retain a record of capital-gain distribution dividends because they must be reported for tax purposes when they are sold.

Insurance Policies: Keep homeowner and automobile policies as long as the statute of limitations in your state, in case someone injured in your home or car files a claim. Other policies should be kept for the duration of the coverage.

Mortgage or other Loan Discharge: as long as you own the property and for 6 years after sale.

Receipts:

> *Clothing:* Until all possibility of return or exchange is past.
>
> *Credit Card Purchases:* until you receive the credit card statement to see that you have been billed correctly; then file according to use (e.g. warranty).
>
> *Home Improvement Costs:* as long as you own the house or 6 years after you have sold the house if reflected in your tax returns.
>
> *Maintenance Costs on House:* only necessary to keep if you plan to sell your house soon. May want to keep as record of names for service people.
>
> *Major purchases:* for the life of the item.
>
> *Medical and other Tax-related Receipts:* generally a cancelled check is adequate proof, unless the nature of the expenses is ambiguous. For example, a cancelled check paid to your physician is adequate evidence that you have paid for specific medical advice, but a check to the drugstore will need supporting evidence to prove that it was a medical expense.

Rent Receipts: cancelled checks will serve as proof of payment.

Utility Bills: 2 years (if kept to compare year-to-year expense, or for home-resale information).

Warranties and Directions: warranties until they expire; directions for the life of the item described.

Index

THE "TO DO" BOOK

MAIL TO: Barbara Hemphill Associates • Suite 410 • 1718 Connecticut Avenue • Washington, D.C. 20009 • (202) 387-8007

NAME _____

ADDRESS _____

CITY _____ STATE ____ ZIP ____

___ (No.) of books at $12 $___
Shipping and Handling
1 book $1.75
2 books $2.90
3 books or more $1 x ___ books $___
Virginia residents add 4½% tax $___
TOTAL ENCLOSED $___

☐ Check here for information about our seminars.
☐ Check here for more information about Barbara Hemphill Associates.

Charge to my ___ VISA or to my ___ MASTERCARD Account.

Name _____   _____
(Please Print)   Account No.

_____   _____
Signature   Expiration Date

THE DAILY PLANNER

MAIL TO: Barbara Hemphill Associates • Suite 410 • 1718 Connecticut Avenue • Washington, D.C. 20009 • (202) 387-8007

NAME _____

ADDRESS _____

CITY _____ STATE ____ ZIP ____

___ (No.) of books at $10 $___
Shipping and Handling
1 Calendar $1.75
2 Calendars $2.90
3 Calendars or more $1 ea $___
Virginia residents add 4½% tax $___
TOTAL ENCLOSED $___

Charge to my ___ VISA or ___ MASTERCARD Account.

Name _____   _____
(Please Print)   Account No.

_____   _____
Signature   Expiration Date